Front Line USA
Threats, Attacks, Arrests and Harassment of Human Rights Defenders

Edited by Paul Hoffman

Researched and Written by John Rendler

Published by Front Line,
16 Idrone Lane, Off Bath Place, Blackrock, Co. Dublin, Ireland

ISBN 0-9547883-0-3
This report is available at a cost of €15 (plus postage and packing).

Preface

"We ask you for solidarity – not action in support of us for that would be inappropriate: but understanding that we are as isolated as you are"
— Lynne Stewart, International conference of human rights defenders, Dublin 2003.

Front Line – The International Foundation for the Protection of Human Rights Defenders decided to commission a report on the situation of human rights defenders in the USA for two main reasons. Firstly there was concern that in the aftermath of 9/11 the measures introduced in the context of the "war on terror" were having a negative impact on human rights defenders and their work in the USA. We felt that this required further investigation. Secondly we felt that there were important linkages between the way the "war on terror" was being used to repress the work of human rights defenders internationally and measures that were being taken within the US. Flowing from this we felt that it would be helpful to try to promote greater international understanding of the challenges faced by human rights defenders within the US and to facilitate links between them and human rights defenders internationally.

The report details the challenges facing those working for human rights in specific areas, which include discrimination, harassment, intimidation, death threats, ill treatment, arrest and detention, spurious legal actions and loss of earnings. The conclusions of the report highlight the fact that over the past two years, human rights defenders in the USA have become increasingly vulnerable to repressive consequences as a result of their human rights activities.

The twelve cases of Human Rights Defenders were chosen to reflect the broad range of issues on which human rights defenders are working in the USA and the different kinds of difficulties they face. Whilst Front Line supports their work our specific focus is on the security and protection of human rights defenders themselves. There was also a conscious attempt to get a reasonable geographic spread across the country.

The report was written and researched by John Rendler, former Executive Director of Minnesota Advocates for Human Rights. The report was reviewed and portions of it edited by Paul Hoffman.

The report was launched in Washington DC on June 9th 2004 in association with the Robert F. Kennedy Memorial Center for Human Rights. Front Line would like to thank all those at the Center for all their help with the launch and for all their ongoing work on behalf of human rights defenders.

It was reviewed by Professor Charles Henry, Department of African American Studies, University of California at Berkeley, Professor David Cole of Georgetown University Law School and Andrew Anderson Deputy Director of Front Line.

The views expressed in this Report are those of Front Line and no other organization.

Front Line
May 2004

Acknowledgements

This report would not have been possible without the input, help and advice of many people. It is important firstly to acknowledge the human rights defenders themselves, their families and colleagues, and all those who helped us to bring their stories together in this report.

Nancy Flowers contributed her editorial expertise, her vast understanding of international and US human rights, and her support and encouragement. This report would not have been possible without her work.

Thanks also to Charles Henry in Berkeley and David Cole in Georgetown for their careful review and perceptive comments.

James Mehigan was responsible for proofing and formatting the text. The report was printed by Blackrock Printers.

John Rendler acknowledges his heartfelt appreciation and admiration to Ruth Barrett Rendler for her constant support, patient understanding and wise advice.

Thanks also to Marianne Philbin in Chicago and Adrienne Quarry at Notre Dame for their help with the research.

Contents

List of Abbreviations   viii

Notes on Contributors   x

Executive Summary   1

Recommendations   5

Human Rights Defenders

    Farouk Abdel-Muhti, New York City   9

    The Coalition of Imokalee Workers, Immokalee, Florida   19

    Carrie and Mary Dann, Western Shoshone Nation (Nevada)   31

    Jeff Dietrich, Los Angeles, California   45

    Brenda and Wanda Henson, Ovett, Mississippi   57

    Cheri Honkala, Philadelphia   69

    Chokwe Lumumba   81

       Detroit, Michigan and Jackson, Mississippi

    Enrique Morones, San Diego, California   93

    Ken Riley and the Charleston Five   103

       Charleston, South Carolina

    Lynne Stewart, New York City   113

    Charles Tisdale, Jackson, Mississippi   125

    James Yee, Fort Benning, Georgia   137

Analysis, Conclusions and Recommendations   151

Conclusion   169

Appendix I: United Nations Declaration on the Rights and Responsibilities of Individuals, Groups and Organs of Society to Promote and Protect Universally Recognized Human Rights and Fundamental Freedoms   171

Appendix II: Additional International Protections   181

Appendix III: Special Representative of the Secretary General on human rights defenders.   187

Abbreviations

ACHR	American Convention on Human Rights
ACLU	American Civil Liberties Union
AEDPA	Anti-Terrorism and Effective Death Penalty Act of 1996
AFL-CIO	American Federation of Labor – Congress of Industrial Organizations
AMR	Agreement of Mutual Responsibility
ATF	Department of Alcohol, Tobacco, and Firearms
CCI	Capital Center Improvement Group
CERD	Convention to Eliminate Racial Discrimination
CIA	Central Intelligence Agency
CIW	Coalition of Immokalee Workers
DARPA	Defense Advanced Research Projects Agency
DOJ	Department of Justice
FBI	Federal Bureau of Investigation
FISC	Foreign Intelligence Surveillance Court
HQPDU	INS Headquarters Post-Order Detention Unit
HUD	Department of Housing and Urban Development
IACHR	Inter-American Commission on Human Rights
ICC	Indian Claims Commission
ICCPR	International Covenant on Civil and Political Rights
ICESCR	International Covenant on Economic, Social and Cultural Rights
IDC	International Dockworkers' Council
ILO	International Labor Organization
INS	Immigration and Naturalization Service
JTTF	Joint Terrorism Task Force
KWRU	Kensington Welfare Rights Union
NGO	Non-Governmental Organization
NMD	National Missile Defense
PATRIOT Act	Full title is USA PATRIOT Act, Uniting and Strengthening America by Providing Appropriate Tools Required to Intercept and Obstruct Terrorism
RNA	Republic of New Afrika
SCLC	Southern Christian Leadership Conference
SNCC	Student National Coordinating Committee
SUV	Sports Utility Vehicle

TANF	Temporary Assistance to Needy Families
TIA	Terrorism Information Awareness formerly the Total Information Awareness Project
TTIC	Terrorist Threat Integration Center
UDHR	Universal Declaration of Human Rights
UN	United Nations
WSDP	Western Shoshone Defense Project
WTO	World Trade Organization

Notes on Contributors

The report was reviewed and edited by Paul Hoffman. Paul Hoffman is a distinguished human rights and civil rights lawyers based in Los Angeles, California. He was for many years the Legal Director of the American Civil Liberties Union (ACLU) Foundation of Southern California. He has been actively involved in the work of several human rights organizations, including Amnesty International and Human Rights Watch, and has taught international human rights law at several U.S. law schools and at Oxford University.

The report was researched and written by John Rendler who has been a human rights advocate for over 25 years. Since 1980, he has held both volunteer leader and staff positions with Amnesty International USA. In 1994, he worked with Unicef in Zaire and Rwanda caring for children orphaned by the genocide. From 1997 to 1999, he was executive director of Minnesota Advocates for Human Rights. He is currently a consultant for human rights groups in Asia, Europe and the United States. He resides in Minneapolis with his wife Ruth and daughter Virginia.

Professor David Cole and Professor Charles Henry also reviewed the text.

David Cole is Professor of Law at Georgetown University.

Charles Henry is Professor of African American Studies at the University of California at Berkeley.

Executive Summary

This report presents portraits of twelve human rights defenders in the United States. It provides a sense of the kinds of abuses that such defenders are addressing and chronicles their vulnerability: the ways they are harassed, threatened, intimidated, and abused as a direct consequence of their work.

These advocates work to promote and protect fundamental human freedoms in the USA — political, civil, economic, social and cultural. They also protect and advance the lives and work of other human rights activists. They are fighting to preserve civil and political rights threatened by the "war on terrorism", and to advance the internationally accepted economic and social rights that the US Government consistently refuses to recognize. They are bringing the language, norms, and force of international human rights protections to their work on US domestic abuses.

In addition to being extraordinary individuals, the human rights defenders presented here share some common qualities:

- They are leaders in the defense of human rights in the United States, activists whose commitment, capacity, and courage have led them to become protectors of the rights and the work of other activists.

- They are residents of the United States, working to protect and promote human rights and draw attention to violations and abuses arising within the USA.

- As a direct result of their work, each has experienced negative repercussions and abuses at the hands of the US Government or American society.

The human rights defenders presented in this report are:

Farouk Abdel-Muhti, New Jersey, an advocate for Arab American rights, held in deportation detention for two years.

The Coalition of Immokalee Workers, Immokalee, Florida, threatened and intimidated for their work to protect the rights and the lives of migrant agricultural workers.

Carrie and Mary Dann, Western Shoshone Nation (Nevada), harassed, attacked, and prevented from earning a living by the US Bureau of Land Management for their leadership of the struggle for traditional Native American rights.

Jeff Dietrich, Los Angeles, arrested several times and held in solitary confinement for his peaceful protests against homelessness and US military actions.

Brenda and Wanda Henson, Ovett, Mississippi, continually harassed and attacked because of their efforts to protect the rights of lesbians.

Cheri Honkala, Philadelphia, arrested over eighty times for her efforts to house the homeless and reduce poverty.

Chokwe Lumumba, Jackson, Mississippi, threatened, jailed, and facing disbarment proceedings as a result of his work for racial justice.

Enrique Morones, San Diego, California, fired from his job because of his activities on behalf of the rights of Latinos and Mexican immigrants.

Ken Riley and the Charleston Five, Charleston, South Carolina, dock workers beaten by police, detained and placed under house arrest after demonstrating for labor rights.

Lynne Stewart, New York City, facing US Department of Justice charges of "providing material support" to terrorists in consequence of her legal defense of Sheik Abdel Rahman.

Charles Tisdale, Jackson, Mississippi, publisher of the *Jackson Advocate* newspaper, threatened with death over 100 times, his office firebombed as a result of his efforts to advance the rights of African Americans.

US Army Captain James Yee, Olympia, Washington, the former Muslim chaplain at the US detention facility at Guantanamo Bay, held without charge on suspicion of 'espionage'.

Taken together, these US human rights defenders provide leadership in the effort to promote and protect basic freedoms such as:

- The threat to fundamental rights resulting from the "war on terrorism".
- The right to adequate food and shelter.
- The rights of immigrants.
- Freedom from arbitrary detention.
- Humane prison conditions.
- Freedom from discrimination on the basis of race, religion, sexual identity, class, or nationality.
- Freedom of expression and of the press.
- Labor and employment rights.
- The right to peaceful assembly and protest.
- The right to adequate legal representation.
- Abolition of the death penalty.

In the profiles of the twelve defenders, several themes emerge:

- Restrictions on basic human rights are increasing as a result of legal and administrative regulations associated with the "war on terrorism".
- Racial prejudice continues to be the paramount American social sickness. Formal segregation and Jim Crow laws may be gone, but racism and discrimination – both subtle and blatant – still exist.
- Increasingly, human rights defenders are confronting violations by private security and paramilitary personnel.
- Solitary confinement and sensory deprivation are used far more often than is generally recognized; such punishment appears to be even more likely if the prisoner has been charged with an offense that has political content.

4

- There is a need for additional human rights protections for people living outside the traditional norms of US society: the poor and homeless; undocumented immigrants; prisoners; Muslims; gay, lesbian and transgender individuals and couples; Native Americans.
- Human rights defenders are devoting substantial and growing attention to economic and social rights, and developing a greater appreciation among activists for the integrity and interdependence of all human rights.
- A growing number of human rights activists have deepened and broadened their capacity and commitment to become defenders of the rights of other activists.
- New motivation, new strategies, and new ways of thinking have been created by adopting and adapting international human rights language, guarantees, and protections to US domestic abuses and by appealing to international human rights forums about violations in the United States.
- There is a need for recognition of, cooperation with, and protection of human rights defenders.

It is our hope that this report will serve to emphasize the importance of the role of human rights defenders to the protection and promotion of basic freedoms in the United States and around the world. We hope that the profiles of the defenders presented here will be a source of ideas and give a sense of solidarity to all human rights defenders. And we hope that their lives and work will inspire and motivate a new generation of human rights defenders.

Recommendations

Front Line believes that the case studies in this Report reflect the kinds of challenges that many human rights defenders face in their work in the United States. Though human rights defenders enjoy a wide range of protections in the United States, the promises made in the Human Rights Defender Declaration are not uniformly respected and further action needs to be taken to make these promises a universal reality for all human rights defenders in the United States.

The work of these human rights defenders also reveals the gaps in human rights protection in the United States more generally. This is especially true for the most vulnerable segments of American society. Though US law provides many human rights protections, the United States has not taken seriously its commitment to the universal and indivisible international human rights standards set forth in the Universal Declaration of Human Rights and the body of international human rights treaties the international community has agreed on since World War Two. In particular, the United States refuses to recognize international economic, social and cultural rights as rights.

Thus, Front Line starts with a recommendation that all levels of government in the United States take steps to fully implement the rights recognized in the human rights treaties the United States has ratified and to complete the process of ratification and implementation of the full range of civil, political, economic, social and cultural rights promised by the Universal Declaration of Human Rights. All persons in the United States will enjoy greater protection and freedoms if such steps are taken.

With respect to human rights defenders, in particular, Front Line makes the following recommendations based on the research in this Report:

1. At all levels of government in the USA, federal, state and local, steps should be taken to implement the protections in the UN Human Rights Defenders Declaration. These steps should include legislative, administrative and judicial actions.

2. The Civil Rights Division of the US Justice Department should use its existing powers to investigate allegations of violations of the rights of

human rights defenders and should seek additional authority and resources to the extent necessary to ensure that the protections in the Human Rights Defender Declaration are fulfilled.

3. Other federal agencies (e.g. the Department of Homeland Security) should take similar steps to ensure that the rights of human rights defenders are respected in the course of their activities.

4. Congress should hold hearings on the impact of measures taken in pursuit of the "war against terrorism" (e.g. political surveillance, intrusions on privacy, detention policies) on the work of human rights defenders in the United States and take action to protect human rights defenders in this context.

5. State and local law enforcement and prosecutorial agencies should take similar steps to ensure the fulfillment of the protections in the Human Rights Defender Declaration in their jurisdictions. These actions should include steps to protect human rights defenders from violence and other forms of harassment by private parties as well. As this Report demonstrates, there are some states (e.g. Mississippi) where such actions must be undertaken on an urgent basis.

6. The U.S. Civil Rights Commission should investigate the extent to which the protections in the Human Rights Defenders Declaration are being fulfilled within the United States and should recommend legislative and administrative reforms to ensure the nationwide implementation of the Declaration.

7. The United States should invite the UN Special Representative for Human Rights Defenders to visit the United States and to report on the state of protections for human rights defenders.

8. Human rights NGOs in other countries should consider taking action in support of human rights defenders at risk in the United States.

9. Human rights NGOs in and outside the United States should consider joint projects and exchanges, ensuring that human rights defenders in the United States become active participants in the international human rights

movement.   Front Line believes that the exchange of experiences across boundaries will benefit all human rights defenders.

Farouk Abdel-Muhti
New York City

"I am deeply sorry for what happened on 9/11 in my city, New York, the victim of this tragedy, and for those who died that day. As the civil rights leader Julian Bond said, 'There was no gender, no race, no religion; it was everyone helping each other'. But now on the streets of the United States again there is gender, there is race, there is religion"
— *Farouk Abdel-Muhti*

Farouk Abdel-Muhti is a 56-year-old stateless Palestinian human rights defender who has been living in the United States since 1975. On April 26, 2002, he was arrested based on a deportation order that had been issued seven years earlier. He was detained without charge until April 12, 2004, much of that time in solitary confinement. He has been interrogated, beaten by law enforcement agents and prison guards, handcuffed and manacled and shackled, held for weeks in a steel cell for twenty-three hours a day, and denied medical care. Front Line is concerned that his detention and treatment was linked to his work to defend human rights.

Over the past thirty years, Abdel-Muhti has been an important human rights activist and advocate on a variety of issues. He has been an influential advocate for the rights of Palestinians in the occupied territories and for Palestinian self-determination; he has campaigned for change in US foreign policy toward the Middle East. Abdel-Muhti supports a two-state solution that would allow an independent Palestine to co-exist alongside Israel, a position which places him in the mainstream of Palestinian opinion. He has been clear that he does not support terrorism or violence.

In the months following the terrorist attacks of September 11, 2001, he spoke and wrote tirelessly in defense of the human rights of Muslims in the USA. He has organized, trained, and motivated many individuals and organizations involved in pressing for the rights of immigrants. He has led opposition to the US military's practice of running test bombing raids on the Puerto Rican island of Vieques. He has helped organize and unionize workers to fight sweatshop conditions in New York City's garment district, and organized assistance for Salvadorans injured on non-union work sites.

Even now he is advocating on behalf of the rights of other activists who are detained and facing deportation.

The USA has not been able to deport Abdel-Muhti because he is stateless. The Office of Detention and Removal, of the Bureau of Immigration and Customs Enforcement, of the Department of Homeland Security, of the United States Government, has tried and failed to send him out of the country because there is no place for him to go. Like most Palestinians in the USA, he has no country where he can assert citizenship or claim residence. He has cooperated with the Government in this process, has not attempted to impede his removal, and has provided the Immigration and Naturalization Service (INS) with proof of his identity and nationality.[1]

* * *

Farouk Abdel-Muhti was born in 1947 in Ramallah in what is now the West Bank. As a teenager in the 1960s, he left for Central America and never returned. He entered the USA from Mexico in 1975.

In 1988, when Jordan's King Hussein abandoned his claims to the West Bank "and its people", Abdel-Muhti and other Palestinians born there but no longer in residence lost their rights to claim Jordanian citizenship or to establish a residence there. Jordan issues "temporary transit passports" to West Bank Palestinians if they possess Israeli residence permits for the area. But since Abdel-Muhti had emigrated before the Israeli takeover in 1967 and has not been in residence there since then, He is not eligible for even a temporary Jordanian passport. Nor does Abdel-Muhti qualify for Palestinian National Authority passport because he left Palestine before the 1993 Oslo accords. In his teenage years, he lived with an uncle in Honduras but without status and thus cannot claim citizenship or residence there. All these nations have refused him travel documents.

In 1995 an INS judge issued a deportation order against Abdel-Muhti because he was "out of status", being in the country without travel documents. He was held for thirteen months at the INS processing center in lower Manhattan before being released on bail. For the next six years while

---

[1] Unless otherwise noted, material on this case was obtained from interviews with Farouk Abdel-Muhti's attorneys, others with information on the case or Abdel-Muhti's life, and legal briefs filed by Abdel-Muhti and the US government.

his case apparently stalled, he lived peacefully and without incident. Throughout his time in the USA, Abdel-Muhti has been an advocate for respecting the rights of the Palestinian people — those in the USA as well as those in the Middle East.

In January 2002 the US Department of Justice issued a directive entitled the "Absconder Apprehension Initiative". The directive instructed agents to arrest immigrants who had ignored deportation orders, with priority attention to over 6000 such cases of immigrants from "Arab" countries.

In the first few months of 2002, Abdel-Muhti increased the intensity of his human rights work. He began publishing and disseminating information on the rights of immigrants. He assisted in organizing demonstrations for the rights of Palestinians, including a notable event at the UN. In March Abdel-Muhti began doing volunteer work at the New York radio station WBAI FM. He arranged and sometimes translated interviews with residents and aid groups in the occupied territories. At that time the Israeli Defense Forces were pursuing a particularly punishing campaign of village incursions and mass detentions of Palestinians. WBAI provided extensive coverage that was openly critical of Israeli and US policy. In April, Abdel-Muhti was a speaker before large crowds in Washington, DC, demonstrating in support of Palestinians and in opposition to civil liberties violations inherent in the "war on terrorism".

At 5:45 on the morning of April 26, 2002, Abdel-Muhti was arrested by two New York City police detectives and a federal agent at an apartment where he and his son were houseguests. Tarek Abdel-Muhti, a US citizen, was 14 years old at the time. Farouk asked through the closed door if the officers had a warrant, to which they replied, "We don't need a ******* warrant. You've got explosives in there". The police threatened to storm the apartment with a SWAT team. When Farouk opened the door, the officers rushed in, cut the phone line, and took Farouk away in handcuffs.

Abdel-Muhti was taken to the INS headquarters in New York where he was interrogated by two FBI agents. They asked him if he had ties to Al Qaeda, Hamas, or the Holy Land Foundation. They asked him to provide names of people who contributed money to Palestinians in the occupied territories. At this point Abdel-Muhti says that the agents threatened to turn him over to the Israeli secret service agency Mossad, one of the agents slapped him in the face and knocked him to the floor, and three INS agents came in and beat him for fifteen minutes. A spokesman for the New York office of Homeland Security said that he was "unable to confirm the allegations".[2]

Abdel-Muhti was initially imprisoned at Middlesex County Jail, transferred a short time later to the Camden County Jail, and then again to the Passaic County Jail, all in New Jersey.

* * *

In November of 2002, Abdel-Muhti's attorneys filed a habeas corpus petition demanding that the Government release him based on the Supreme Court's 2001 decision in Zadvydas v. Davis. Before this decision detention for stateless persons was, in effect, permanent. In the Zadvydas opinion, the US Supreme Court set out certain conditions for the detention of individuals the Government intends to deport. After being detained for six months, if the individual can demonstrate that there is no likelihood of removal in the reasonably foreseeable future, he or she must be released.

In Abdel-Muhti's case US Government contended that the six-month period would not start until he cooperated and provided conclusive proof of his identity, birthplace, and citizenship. Abdel-Muhti's legal team says that the Government's claims are wrong on three counts. First, the team has "diligently cooperated" with US efforts to remove him from the country and have provided authorities with all the proof of identity that Abdel-Muhti possesses, including a birth certificate issued in Jordan showing that he was born in Ramallah and an affidavit from a family friend who recalls Abdel-Muhti's birth. Second, Abdel-Muhti has asserted that he is willing to be deported, but neither his attorneys nor the US Government have been able to secure travel documents from any nation; and since he is literally a "man without a country", continuing such efforts is "futile". Third, the Government has no right to place an arbitrary date on when his six months of detention begins; logic dictates that the clock should have started when he was arrested.[3]

[2] Jordan Green, 'Silencing Dissent', *ColorLines Magazine*, Summer 2003.

[3] Farouk Abdel-Muhti, petitioner, vs. Tom Ridge, Secretary, Department of Homeland Security; Michael Garcia, Asst Secretary for the Bureau of Immigration and Customs Enforcement; Patricia Mullin, Head, Bureau of Immigration and Customs Enforcement for the District of Philadelphia; David Venturella, Asst Deputy Executive Associate Commissioner, Office of Detention and Removal, Bureau of Immigration and

The Supreme Court also noted that as the period of detention grows longer, deportation must become more realistic and more imminent; if this is not the case, the detainee should be released. Attorneys for Abdel-Muhti argued that not only was deportation not imminent and not realistic, it was "inconceivable", and therefore the Government has no choice but to release him. The Court placed the burden of proof on the detainee — he or she must make a good-faith effort to demonstrate that there is no place to go. But the detainee does not have to prove that it is completely impossible for him to be repatriated.[4]

Responding to the Supreme Court's ruling, the US Immigration and Naturalization Service (INS) established rules and procedures for people in Abdel-Muhti's situation. The detainee must apply to the INS Headquarters Post-Order Detention Unit (HQPDU), affirming that "there is no significant likelihood that the alien will be removed in the reasonably foreseeable future to the country to which the alien was ordered removed and there is no third country willing to accept the alien". The assertion must be accompanied by "information sufficient to establish his or her compliance with the obligation to effect his or her removal and to cooperate in the process of obtaining necessary travel documents".[5]

Abdel-Muhti's attorneys have attempted to satisfy these regulations by making approaches to the Jordanian Consulate in Washington, DC; the Palestinian Liberation Organization Mission; the Honduran Consulate; the Egyptian consulate; and the Israeli Consulate in New York City. Briefs filed on behalf of Abdel-Muhti contain correspondence demonstrating that all refused to issue travel documents or residence permits.

Abdel-Muhti's legal teams also argues that the US Government has not done its part to seek travel documents, citing various court rulings that the INS must make "regular efforts to obtain travel documents" and demonstrate "concrete evidence of progress" if continued incarceration is to be justified. Moreover, the attorneys assert that it has been clear to the INS since 1975

Customs Enforcement; Thomas Hogan, Warden, York County Jail, York, Pennsylvania, respondents (legal brief in support of petition for habeas corpus submitted in the United States District Court for the Middle District of Pennsylvania).

[4] Abdel-Muhti v USA.

[5] Abdel-Muhti v USA.

   that Abdel-Muhti is a Palestinian, citing a deportation order from that year
and a deportation notice from 1982 that both say "Palestine" as the
destination of his removal.

* * *

In January 2003, while imprisoned at Passaic, Abdel-Muhti and five other
Muslim immigration detainees staged a hunger strike, demanding that he be
released and that his fellow prisoners be transferred to a facility where they
could have contact visits with their families. The INS agreed to move the
five, but denied Abdel-Muhti's request. An INS spokesman called the
hunger strike "disruptive behavior". Jane Guskin of the Coalition for the
Human Rights of Immigrants said, "But it's the INS that provoked this strike
in the first place. They know that conditions in Passaic are below even their
low standards.... The INS needs to stop criticizing the detainees for taking
this desperate measure and start obeying the law".[6]

On February 19 Abdel-Muhti was himself transferred but to a place he had
no desire to be – York County Prison in southeastern Pennsylvania, 200
miles away from his family, his attorneys and his supporters. MacDonald
Scott, a member of his legal team said, "This transfer interferes with
Farouk's constitutional right to legal representation. The removal so far from
the venue where his case is being heard goes against his due process rights".
The transfer caused a six-month delay in the progress of the case.

At the York County Prison, Abdel-Muhti was housed in a maximum-
security segregation unit. Each of the sixteen prisoners in this unit is kept
isolated in a cell with steel doors for twenty-three hours and fifteen minutes
every day, with forty-five minutes allotted to bathing and making phone
calls. Anytime one of these prisoners is taken from his cell, including for
medical treatment at the clinic, he is handcuffed, shackled, and chained.
Reading material and phone calls are monitored and controlled. When
investigators questioned the solitary confinement, the prison officials at
York claimed it was ordered by the INS. The INS said it was York's
decision

---

[6] David L. Wilson, 'INS Attempts to Break Hunger Strike in Passaic Jail', *Life of Liberty*, 18 January
2003.

At the time Abdel-Muhti said, "I am very disappointed because the INS destroys my rights".

On February 28 the Bush Administration announced that the INS would be merged with the newly created Department of Homeland Security, a cabinet-level office established in response to the "war against terrorism".

On October 9 Abdel-Muhti's legal team filed an updated brief with the US Middle District of Pennsylvania. On October 20, the judge issued an order for the Government to explain its reasons for the continued detention by November 9.

On October 30 Abdel-Muhti was again transferred, this time from York to the Bergen County Jail in Hackensack, New Jersey. On November 19 two corrections officers at Bergen found "leftist publications" in his cell. Abdel-Muhti says they then pushed, kicked, and punched him, called the literature "anti-government", told him to "shut the **** up" and "go back to Palestine". The guards confiscated his personal belongings, including papers, address books and medicine. Abdel-Muhti's attorneys have filed complaints about all these abuses; litigation will continue now that he is released.

On November 25 he was moved to an isolation cell, apparently in consequence of the publications and in anticipation of a celebration at the end of Ramadan. Between November 19 and 25, prison officials withheld all medication from Abdel-Muhti, who suffers from hypertension, arthritis, and a thyroid condition.

On December 5 Abdel-Muhti was transferred again, this time from Bergen to Hudson County Correctional Center in Kearny, New Jersey. Immigration officials refused to respond to his inquiries about where he was being taken and what was going to happen to him, and they failed to notify his attorneys of the transfer. Hudson thus became his sixth prison facility in twenty-two months of confinement.

Living conditions, food, and medical care are notoriously substandard at Hudson, and it is difficult to arrange for contact visits with anyone besides immediate family members. In fact, it is one of the many ironies of US prisons that while violent criminals in state prisons are allowed contact visits, immigration detainees in county jails and federal facilities are denied them. Moreover, most county jails use a telephone system known as "Prison Collect", which charges an exorbitant five dollars for the first minute of conversation and eighty cents for each additional minute.

As Jane Guston says, "The prison system is unfair to all prisoners, but for immigration detainees it's absurd". And Abdel-Muhti's attorneys point out a fundamental flaw in the adjudication of immigration cases: state and federal courts tend to defer to the decisions of immigration courts; and immigration courts defer to the advice of the executive branch: the INS and the Department of Homeland Security.

On February 4, 2004, the US filed a response claiming that Abdel-Muhti's continued detention was warranted because he had not "cooperated" with his own deportation. The Government suggested that Abdel-Muhti should be more active in trying to obtain travel documents, but it offered no suggestions as to how he could possibly do so. Many of Abdel-Muhti's supporters believe that what the Government really means by cooperation is information that might lead to further arrests of Arab-American activists.

* * *

After the September 11, 2001, attacks on New York and Washington, the resulting climate of fear, the increased security represented by the PATRIOT Act, and the escalation of The Bush Administration's rhetoric on the Middle East have increased the vulnerability of Palestinian refugees, especially those Palestinians who were activists and advocates.

Professor David Cole of Georgetown University Law School says, "I've been involved with politically motivated immigration cases for the past twenty years. The vast majority of them have been Arab-American activists. There is a history of the FBI paying more attention to Palestinians and using their activism to deport them when there is no evidence of criminal wrongdoing".[7]

---

[7] Green.

The United Nations Declaration on Human Rights Defenders[8] acknowledges "the valuable work of individuals, groups and associations in contributing to, the effective elimination of all violations of human rights and fundamental freedoms of peoples and individuals, including in relation to...all forms of racial discrimination, colonialism, foreign domination or occupation...and from the refusal to recognize the right of peoples to self-determination". Article 6(b) of the Declaration states that "Everyone has the right, individually and in association with others, as provided for in human rights and other applicable international instruments, freely to publish, impart or disseminate to others views, information and knowledge on all human rights and fundamental freedoms".

The intensified threat of deportation and detention has taken its toll on Palestinian activism and human rights advocacy. Activists are more and more reluctant to speak out; advocates have shifted their attention from protecting the rights of activists in public to protecting them in prison. Abdel-Muhti has tried to do both. Within the prisons where he has been held, he organized, taught and motivated the detained activists around him. From these prisons, he has issued a steady stream of reports, opinions, thoughts, advice, and encouragement to activists still outside.

Abdel-Muhti's supporters contend that he was held for so long because of his non-violent advocacy for an equitable solution to the conflict between the Palestinian nation and the state of Israel. They considered him to have been a political prisoner. They do not believe it was coincidental that, after living in the US for over twenty-five years, he was arrested and imprisoned six months after the September 11 attacks and a month after he brought his advocacy to the airwaves via a prominent New York radio station. And it does seem unlikely that the Government was unaware that he was not deportable when they arrested him in the first place.

To Arab-American activists, immigration reform advocates, and anyone concerned about the erosion of civil liberties in the United States, Farouk Abdel-Muhti is cause for both heartache and hope. His arrest, imprisonment, and treatment are illustrative of the kind of denigration that Arab-American activists and refugees who are advocates have come to expect from the INS

---

[8] See Appendix I for full title and text of the Human Rights Defenders Declaration

and its successor agencies. In the last two and a half years it has gotten worse by the day.

But on April 8, 2004, in Harrisburg, Pennsylvania, Federal District Judge Yvette Kane issued an order directing the US Government to release Abdel-Muhti within ten days. The court found that the Government had failed to inform him of anything further he needed to do to facilitate his removal from the country.

Judge Kane called the Government's periodic demands for more information about his identity "a Kafkaesque exchange".

Lead counsel for the defense Shayana Kadidal of the Center for Constitutional Rights said, "Farouk was clearly targeted for arrest because of his political activism and outspokenness. Throughout his detention he was harassed and targeted by guards and prison and immigration officials because of his activism".

Three days before the court's decision, supporters and attorneys lost contact with Abdel-Muhti. Not until the afternoon of April 9 was he able to make one five-minute phone call to inform friends that he had been moved to a federal penitentiary in Atlanta, Georgia, over 800 miles from his family and legal team. Finally, at around 10 in the evening of April 12, Abdel-Muhti arrived at New York's La Guardia Airport as a free man. He said, "We won a victory but still have to win the war for justice, equality and rights for both immigrants and all the people in the nation who are fighting for democratic rights and social justice".

Farouk Abdel-Muhti spent 718 days in immigration detention including over 250 days in solitary confinement.

The Coalition of Imokalee Workers
Immokalee, Florida

"We are not talking about 'slavery-like conditions' or 'virtual slavery' in quotation marks. We are speaking of actual slavery according to federal court verdicts, of being held against one's will through violence or threats of violence. The details of the operations investigated by the Coalition of Immokalee Workers leave little room for doubt that slavery, true slavery, still exists in the United States in the 21st century"
- Coalition of Immokalee Workers

The Coalition of Immokalee Workers (CIW) provides an umbrella of protection and advocacy for victims of forced labor, activists who are trying to end such abuses, and Americans across the country who support such efforts. CIW fights slavery and other violations of the rights of field workers by uncovering, investigating, and assisting in federal prosecutions of labor contractors and employers.

Their efforts have improved the status and wellbeing of farm workers along the East Coast of the United States. They fought for and won the first wage rise in over twenty years for thousands of tomato field workers from Pennsylvania to Florida. Over the last six years, they have uncovered and spurred prosecution of five slavery operations resulting in the liberation of over 1000 workers.[9]

CIW's anti-slavery campaign engages in investigations of specific farms, labor camps, labor contractors, and employers, and seeks to eliminate the market conditions that allow slavery to continue. CIW is southeast regional coordinator for the national Freedom Network Institute on Human Trafficking, and provides training for state and federal law enforcement agencies, social service personnel, and community organizations on how to recognize and assist workers suffering human rights abuses.

---

[9] Unless otherwise noted, material for this section was obtained from interviews with members of the Coalition for Immokalee Workers, testimony before the Subcommittee on Human Rights and Wellness of the Government Reform Committee in the US House of Representatives in 2003 and testimony before the Government Reform Committee, Subcommittee on Human Rights and Wellness, US House of Representatives, 28 October 2004.

In December 2002 the *St. Petersburg Times* of St. Petersburg, Florida, called the work of the CIW a "modern day underground railroad", referring to the avenues of escape for African slaves in 18th and 19th century America.[10]

* * *

Lucas Benitez, a founder of the CIW, was born in Guerrero, Mexico, the second of six children. His parents were subsistence farmers in the highlands of Guerrero. He immigrated to the USA when he was 17, hoping to earn enough money to support the family. In 1994 he found himself in Immokalee, Florida, picking oranges and tomatoes. He began to hold meetings with Guatemalan, Haitian, and other Mexican workers discussing basic causes of their demeaning conditions and ways to improve them. Benitez says, "When one of my bosses threatened to beat me up, I was alone in confronting him because of the overwhelming climate of fear in the fields. We wanted to make sure no one would ever be alone again". Those conversations and that organizing of one farm led to the formation of the Coalition of Immokalee Workers in 1995.

The CIW has now become a powerful organization with 2000 members, enough to assure a network that can report on field conditions throughout the USA. They organized the first general strike in Immokalee when 3000 workers walked out of the fields for a week. They organized a boycott of the Taco Bell fast-food chain, demanding accountability for labor abuses among its suppliers. They have created what Benitez calls "a new farm worker community in Immokalee: a community aware of its human rights and active in its own defense—in short, a community that fights back".

Violence is endemic to agricultural slavery enterprises. The CIW faces frequent threats, harassment, intimidation, and physical abuse. Many CIW members have been field workers subjected to forced labor, debt bondage, and slavery. CIW workers have received death threats from labor contractors and employers and have been followed and staked out at their office and homes. Investigative workers have been held at gunpoint.

* * *

---

[10] John Bowe: 'Nobodies: Does Slavery Exist in America?' *The New Yorker*, 21 April 2003.

Julia Gabriel is a Mayan from Guatemala who originally entered the USA as a farm worker in Arizona. In 1992, having heard that there was better work in South Carolina, she accepted her potential employer's offer of transportation. On arrival, however, she found herself in a virtual labor camp. She was told that she owed her employer for the transportation and that she and the others in the camp would be killed if they tried to escape.

Gabriel and her fellow workers in the camp harvested cucumbers twelve hours a day, seven days a week, and were under armed guard twenty-four hours a day. From her week's pay, the employer deducted money for rent, food, transportation, and incidentals, leaving her with only twenty dollars.

The "employers" were in fact a slavery ring overseeing four hundred workers in Georgia and Florida as well as South Carolina. The workers were physically abused and the women sexually abused. Relatives and activists seeking entry to the camps were beaten and shot at.

Another worker told Gabriel, "In the USA you don't have to work by force". The employers gave him a merciless and public "message beating" as a warning to others. Shortly afterward Gabriel and six other workers escaped into the countryside. A few hours to the east, they were hired to pick tomatoes. Benitez quotes Gabriel as saying that she was "making only enough to get by, but we were free, no one beat us, and we could go to the store or the laundromat whenever we wanted to".

When CIW activists visited the tomato camp, Gabriel told them about the slavery operation, joined CIW, and participated in an investigation of the South Carolina cucumber camp. She returned to the camp hidden in the van of a friend. When they arrived, the employer told Gabriel's friend that if he didn't leave immediately he would be shot to death.

After five years of investigation and pressure on the US Government, in 1997 the Department of Justice arrested and prosecuted the employers in a case known as US v. Flores. Gabriel testified in secret to a federal grand jury; the employers pled guilty and she also testified at the sentencing hearing. The defendants each received fifteen year sentences, the longest ever given for such an offense.

US v Flores has become a landmark case in the development of US law on agricultural slavery and forced labor. It spurred the creation of the Government's Worker Exploitation Task Force in 1998 and the Victims of Trafficking and Violence Protection Act in 2001, the first anti-slavery legislation in the USA since 1865.

In a long and significant article in *The New Yorker* magazine, Journalist John Bowe recounts how in the spring of 1998 Gabriel went on to assist the Department of Justice on a slavery case in West Palm Beach, Florida. Rogerio Cadena and several of his relatives were charged with entrapping and smuggling twenty women from Mexico into the USA. The women were held in sexual slavery in trailers that served as brothels, frequented by agricultural workers for twenty dollars a visit. The women were required to perform twenty sex acts each day. At the end of each night, the women turned in their condom wrappers; each wrapper was supposed to contribute toward the paying off of a debt. But they never knew how much they owed or received any indication that their debt was being reduced. Women who escaped were recaptured and returned to face rape and imprisonment. Those who became pregnant were forced to have abortions, and the cost was added to their debt. Gabriel counseled victims who were afraid to confront their employers. They eventually testified and the operators received fifteen year sentences in the case US v Cardena.[11]

* * *

Immokalee, Florida is a town of about 20,000 people eighty-eight miles inland from the Gulf of Mexico. It is bordered by tomato fields and orange groves in an area that supplies much of the produce available in the United States in the winter.

In his *New Yorker* article John Bowe describes CIW's offices this way:

> The group's headquarters is a dilapidated storefront on South Third Street, next to the pickup spot where the workers congregate each morning. The paint is peeling off the walls and the carpet is ripped and threadbare. The principal furnishings include a lumpy old couch, two desks, a few dozen metal

---

[11] Bowe.

folding chairs, and a large papier-mâché replica of the Statue of Liberty holding a tomato bucket. The walls are adorned with photographs of protest marches, cartoons depicting labor relations between bosses and workers, and newspaper articles in Spanish, English, and Creole. Migrant workers stream through all day and into the evening, buying tortillas, Jarritos, soft drinks, and mole-sauce mix at the coalition's co-op grocery store. The place has a feel somewhere between a college social club and a Third World political-party branch office. The group's representatives come from Haiti, Mexico, Guatemala, and the United States. They are paid two-hundred and forty-seven dollars a week—slightly more than a farm worker earning minimum wage for a forty-hour week. They live in trailers and shacks, and work seven days a week, and their conversations seldom stray from the subject of workers' rights....[12]

In Immokalee and throughout the Southeast, local growers do not directly hire the field workers they require to tend and harvest crops. Instead they arrange for migrant workers through labor contractors. As far as the workers are concerned, the contractors are their employers, and they travel with them to seasonal crops around the country. The contractors pay the workers and provide — for a fee — food, housing, and transportation; the grower has no direct responsibility for the workers. Still further removed, a distributor buys the produce from the grower. Still further up the chain are a relatively small number of large firms that buy from the distributor. These firms in turn are owned by large conglomerates such as Cargill, Coca-Cola and Pepsico. At the top of the pyramid are the final buyers: McDonald's, Burger King, Taco Bell, and major supermarket chains.

For many workers the greatest threat is not their employers but the US Government's Immigration and Naturalization Service (INS). The more an immigrant works, the more time he or she spends in the USA, the more of a financial and family disaster deportation becomes.

Over a million migrant workers live in the USA, more than half of them illegally. They plant and harvest almost everything that can be grown. Each

---

[12] Bowe.

year approximately 50,000 women and children are illegally, often forcibly, brought into the United States, where most are put to work as domestic and field laborers. Over the past three years, the number of human-trafficking prosecutions has tripled, and there are now 125 ongoing investigations.

CIW says, "Isolated labor camps, overwhelmingly powerful and sometimes violent bosses, recently arrived immigrant workers unaware of their rights and cast out alone to make a living in the harshest of conditions—that is the reality faced by the vast majority of farm workers today in this country. And that is the reality that gives rise to slavery in Florida. Of course slavery is the most extreme of the abuses faced by those who harvest this country's fruit and vegetables. Sweatshop conditions are the everyday reality".

A farm worker's average income is about $7500 per year ($6500 around Immokalee), a figure far below the poverty line in the United States. They have no health insurance and often no health care. They receive no vacation pay and no sick leave. They often do not receive pay for overtime work and are denied the right to organize. They have been excluded from the worker rights contained in the US National Labor Relations Act and the Fair Labor Standards Act. And the difficulty of the work they do can break body and mind.

Field workers typically live in metal trailers next to the crops they are harvesting. They may share such accommodation with ten or twelve other workers; two or three families may live in the same trailer, paying $1000 per month for the privilege. They rarely have heat or air-conditioning, cars or telephones. As cell phones become a commonplace "necessity" in mainstream America, these workers are losing one of their few conveniences: the public phone booth.

CIW states, "It is no exaggeration to say that the multi-billion dollar US fruit and vegetable industry is in fact founded upon the systematic violation of two, if not three, of the most fundamental human rights as defined in the UN Declaration on Human Rights. The right to organize, the rights to fair compensation, and, all too often, the right to work free of forced labor, are routinely violated in the planting, cultivating, and harvesting of produce in this country".

CIW believes that slavery and forced labor in the USA can only be understood and eliminated if it is seen in the context of much larger agricultural labor abuses. Lucas Benitez says, "US agriculture operates in an environment of daily, systematic violation of human rights, and it is within that context that slavery, the most egregious form of labor rights violation, is allowed to flourish…. Only once a more modern, more humane system of labor relations is in place — one in which farm workers' basic labor and human rights, including the right to organize, the right to overtime pay, and the right to a fair wage, are respected without exception—will we be able as a society to eradicate the stain of slavery".

To that end, CIW pressures fast-food chains, the major buyers of farm produce, to take responsibility for bringing growers and workers together. In turn, CIW informs consumers about farm worker abuses and has organized a boycott of the fast-food chain Taco Bell. CIW says,

> If the fast-food industry will employ a tiny portion of its vast resources towards eliminating slavery and other labor abuses in its supply chain, the lives of the millions of farm workers who contribute to fast-food profits will improve swiftly and dramatically. US consumers should demand no less.

CIW has observed:

> In twenty-first century America, slavery remains woven into the fabric of our daily lives. On any given day, the tomatoes in the burgers we eat or the oranges in the juice we drink may have been picked by captive workers. The major buyers of Florida produce—corporations like Taco Bell, McDonalds, Tropicana, Burger King, and Wal-Mart that sell the majority of produce to the public—have a crucial role to play in modernizing working conditions in Florida agriculture. The fast-food industry in particular has grown almost overnight into a multi-billion dollar, multi-national business, thanks in large part to low-cost ingredients that have allowed fast-food chains to control costs and plow their profits back into advertising and expansion. Convictions and harsh sentences for crew leaders who enslave their workers are necessary today because corporate growers and their multi-billion dollar corporate clients continue to

demand cheap labor with little concern given to how labor costs are controlled....We firmly believe...that the struggle will be made infinitely easier, and ultimately won, through an approach that demands more of our country's huge retail food industries than simply turning a blind eye to human rights violations in their supply chain as they profit from high-quality, low-price produce kept cheap through the deprivations of tens of thousands of this country's hardest working men and women, US farm workers.

* * *

In 1999 three tomato field workers escaped from a labor camp in the swamps just outside Immokalee. Their boss found them walking along a road and tried to run them down with his SUV, hitting one of them. The boss then followed them to a CIW member's house and threatened the workers and the CIW member's family, shouting that he had paid for them and owned them. The workers later told CIW that they were held at the camp against their will, forced to work off a $1000 debt that never lessened, and threatened with death. At the prompting of CIW, federal officials raided the camp, freed thirty workers, and charged the employer with conspiracy to hold workers in slavery. In January 2000, the employers pled guilty and were sentenced to prison terms.

In the spring of 2000, a taxi-van pulled up outside a market in Lake Placid, Florida, to pick up several migrant workers and take them out of town. Six armed men attacked the van driver and held the passengers at gunpoint. CIW activists and police sped to the scene and rescued the workers and the driver:

The armed men were from a large family who ran harvesting companies in Florida and North Carolina, with a multi-state reach and level of violence that was extreme. They ran crews of over 800 workers, and controlled every aspect of their lives, including their housing, pay, transportation to and from the groves, and the stores they bought from. They used guards with cell phones to keep constant watch over those who would try to leave. And the one thing they couldn't control fully—taxi-van services coming into town and representing a way to escape for workers—they attacked viciously, and pressured store owners not to sell bus tickets. By closing off the workers' only way out, they effectively put up a fence around people, only it was a fence that law enforcement officials and the general public were unable to see.

One of CIW's activists, a young Guatemalan named Romeo Ramirez, agreed to work undercover at the Lake Placid operation. Ramirez was able to confirm information CIW had received about workers held against their will. On a return visit, Ramirez was recognized by one of the guards; a boss then blocked Ramirez's car with his truck, charged him with trying to "take their people", and threatening him with bodily harm. Ramirez bluffed the boss by acting angry that he had never been paid for the work he'd done.

John Bowe relates how in April 2001, Lucas Benitez and other CIW members drove to Lake Placid to rescue three of the captive workers:

> Around sunset, a white Mercury Grand Marquis with tinted windows pulled off Highway 27, a short distance from [the camp]. Lucas Benitez emerged and raised the hood, as if checking an overheated radiator. From the balcony of a nearby hotel, [CIW activists] Asbed and Germino signaled that the coast was clear. [The workers] sat on a railroad tie at the camp's edge, near the highway, debating what they were about to do. Then, leaving all their belongings, including their Mexican documents, behind, they walked slowly toward the roadside. As they neared the Grand Marquis, they suddenly began sprinting, and jumped into the back seat as Benitez slammed the hood closed, got behind the wheel, and gunned the car down the road. The passengers kept their heads out of view until they were twenty miles away.

Within days the Federal Bureau of Investigation (FBI) interviewed the escaped workers. The labor contractors were arrested and charged with extortion and possession of firearms. As John Bowe reported, the contactor's home was found to conceal "an arsenal of weapons not normally associated with labor management, including a Savage 7mm rifle, an AK-47 semi-automatic rifle, a Browning 9mm semi-automatic pistol, and a Remington 700 7mm rifle". In July of 2002, the contractors were found guilty of slave trafficking and sentenced to a total of thirty-four years in federal prison. They were also ordered to forfeit over three million dollars in assets.

During the investigation and the trial, Benitez was threatened with physical harm if he did not stop CIW's participation on the case. Oversize pickup trucks followed him and circled his home. Sugar was put in his gas tank and roofing nails in his tires. Often when Benitez called the police for help, the threats were not taken seriously. The contactors sent henchmen to Immokalee to make death threats against the owner of the taxi-van service. Associates of the contractors harassed and intimidated witnesses and kept an intimidating presence outside the CIW office.

In February of 2003, as part of their campaign to boycott the Taco Bell fast-food chain, CIW organized one of the biggest hunger strikes in labor history—ten days and nights without food while huddling outside Taco Bell's international corporate headquarters in Irvine, California. They were harassed by local police and denied tents and toilets for most of their vigil; three strikers were hospitalized. The strike ended when national religious leaders pledged to take up their cause and pleaded with them to desist for the sake of their health. The boycott has been covered by the Public Broadcasting System, *The New Yorker*, and *National Geographic*.

* * *

Simply put, members of the Coalition of Immokalee workers go into dangerous situations and rescue people from slavery. That activity gives them notoriety, but it is only a tiny portion of their work. They provide training and education for field workers and activists. They disseminate information about field conditions to US consumers. They pressure Congress to enact the legislation needed to restore the rights of farm workers. Perhaps most important, they have made the struggle of field and farm workers in the Southeast a national and international human rights issue.

The United Nations Declaration on Human Rights Defenders states in Article 5: "For the purpose of promoting and protecting human rights and fundamental freedoms, everyone has the right, individually and in association with others… to meet or assemble peacefully… to form, join and participate in non-governmental organizations, associations or groups".

Article 12 of the Declaration states that "everyone has the right, individually and in association with others, to participate in peaceful activities against violations of human rights and fundamental freedoms;" and,

> The State shall take all necessary measures to ensure the protection by the competent authorities of everyone, individually and in association with others, against any violence, threats, retaliation, *de facto* or *de jure* adverse discrimination, pressure or any other arbitrary action as a consequence of his or her legitimate exercise of the rights referred to in the present Declaration.

The work of CIW has received widespread recognition. CIW received the 2003 Robert F. Kennedy Human Rights Award. Julia Gabriel has been honored with the National Organization for Women's Woman of Courage Award for 2000. In 1999 Lucas Benitez received the Rolling Stone magazine/Brick Award as outstanding young leader. In 1999 and 2000, CIW was instrumental in Congress enacting the Trafficking Victims Protection Act, which makes involuntary servitude a federal felony.

In 2001 the US Commission on Civil Rights issued a report which stated,

> The [South's] unique history of slavery, with its debilitating legacies—the sharecropping system, Jim Crow laws, the concentration of wealth in the hands of a minority white population, the political disenfranchisement of blacks and the nearly total segregation of the races—has been well documented and is generally viewed as the most significant factor in the region's present position as among the poorest, if not the poorest, section of the nation based on virtually every socioeconomic measurement.

Jaribu Hill, Director of The Mississippi Workers' Center for Human Rights, puts it this way:

> It has to be an international human rights struggle. It is not by default that you are poor. It is not because you messed up. It is not by design. You are treated this way because of the historical

system of slavery and human bondage. If we keep the struggle local,
we suffer and don't know why we suffer.

CIW staffer Laura Germino says, "What are you going to do? You can't just
stand there with your arms crossed".

Carrie and Mary Dann
Western Shoshone Nation (Nevada)

"The earth is our mother and we can't give up our mother. No way in hell"
- Carrie Dann

Carrie and Mary Dann are elders of the Western Shoshone Native American nation. For more than thirty years they have struggled to defend land rights and the rights of indigenous peoples. They have faced harassment and the seizure of their cattle and horses. They live in constant fear of being evicted from their land by the US Government. They have been denied justice through the US courts even though the Inter-American Commission of Human Rights has found the US Government in violation of international human rights law in its handling of land disputes with the Western Shoshone. Front Line is concerned that the continued action by the US Government against the Dann sisters and their property is linked to their defense of their people's human rights.

Mary believes she is in her ninth decade, Carrie in her eighth. The sisters speak softly and directly with a profound moral authority. They live together in northeast Nevada in conditions that would seem stark and harsh to most Americans. This is the heart of the American West. Broad plains, high desert and salt flats sweep in all directions to blue and distant mountains. While traditional or extended family members live throughout the area, the Dann homestead is isolated.

Almost by default, certainly without seeking it, the Dann sisters have become the most authoritative and visible advocates for restoring the rights of the Western Shoshone people. They have led the fight of the traditional Shoshone to refuse US Government attempts to force the sale of their land, fearing such payment would mean permanent loss of their ancestral homeland. They have resisted attempts by major mining corporations to develop the land. They have pursued their cause through US courts, political approaches and appeals to international treaty and judicial bodies.

The Danns' income and their way of life depend on their horses and cattle. This livestock depends on access to extensive traditional grazing areas that are now subsumed by so-called "public land", Public land is not land that is open to the public; it is land that is owned or controlled by the US Government. Over eighty percent of the land in Nevada is designated as public land.

In February of 2003, US Bureau of Land Management Rangers swept onto the Danns' traditional grazing land. Armed with automatic weapons, accompanied by other federal agents and local herders, using helicopters, all-terrain vehicles and tractor-trailer trucks, the agents forcibly rounded-up and seized the Danns' horses. In fifteen days, they took away 504 horses — the Danns' livelihood and inheritance from generations past.

Carrie Dann says, "I was indigenous and in one single evening they made me indigent. If you think the Indian wars are over, then think again".[13]

* * *

For hundreds of years the Danns and other Shoshone families have grazed horses over 100,000 acres — two valleys and a mountain range — of traditional Western Shoshone land. For over a century they have defended this land from steady encroachment by both Government and white settlers.

Carrie and Mary Dann live deliberately simple lives. Their house is a bare frame structure paneled with plywood. Heat comes from a wood stove, electricity from a household generator. They do not keep a large stock of food and do not use modern appliances. They are some distance from a paved road and are not connected to power lines. They have a telephone but they don't answer it. Unlike many of their neighbors, the Danns refuse to accept any form of government assistance, making their defiance all the more credible to their supporters and all the more galling to Government agents.

For the Danns and other Shoshone, traditional living means practicing one's beliefs in the sanctity of the earth, the water, the land, the sun and the air.
It means living "close to the earth" with respect for the land and all the creatures upon it. It means bringing honor to your family and to the earth. It is a belief in two mothers — the birth mother and the Earth Mother.

---

[13] Material on Carrie and Mary Dann was obtained from interviews with the Dann sisters on their Nevada ranch in December 2003.

Respect for the land is crucial. Carrie Dann says, "If you damage the Earth Mother, you damage yourself. If you punch holes in the Earth Mother, you punch holes in your soul. If you remove the fluid from Mother Earth, you drain the life from yourself". Carrie Dann says, "As the Earth gives birth to you and nurtures you, so you do with your own children.... our spirituality is not a Sunday sort of thing. It is lived every moment. The Spirits walk side by side with us".

The greatest personal threat to the Danns is the possibility that the US Government will foreclose on their homestead — their home and farm — as a consequence for allegedly unpaid grazing fees. The Danns live in constant fear: of losing their ability to earn a living, of being forced to leave their father's homestead, of leaving the land of their ancestors, of losing their traditional and spiritual way of living.

All Western Shoshone people face the same loss of their ancestral lands and culture. Known in their language as Newe Sogobia, these lands extend from the Snake River in Idaho on the north, south into Death Valley and the Mojave Desert; east from Salt Lake Valley in Utah, and west across most of central Nevada, an area roughly the size of Spain.

Traditional Shoshone do not recognize formal borders; for them, the land is divided only by mountain ranges, rivers and deserts. Boundaries, according to Carrie Dann, are "a white man's description of how the land is cut up. Indigenous people don't see the land in straight lines". Native Americans have always recognized the wisdom of having "joint-use areas" where blending takes place between the traditional homelands of one family and another, one nation and another. And it is clear that the Shoshone conception of mining at that time has been human-scale holes bored in a hill, not the huge operational process of taking down a mountain.

* * *

Recently the US Government has discovered vast deposits of gold, phosphates, and geothermal energy under this land and is exploring the extent of available oil. Federal authorities want to develop these resources; the state of Nevada wants the jobs and economic stimulus such development would create.

The Federal Government plans to devote the geothermal energy to power mining operations, especially the extraction of gold. The traditional land of the Shoshone contains two-thirds of the gold produced in the US; it is the third richest gold field in the world. The principal extractor, Cortez Mining Corporation, estimates that over one billion dollars in gold can be extracted from the same land where the Dann's horses graze. Cortez Mining's logo, the famous helmeted profile of the conquistador, can be found on t-shirts, caps and pins throughout the area.

Contracts for developing Western Shoshone land have been given to some of the same corporations now engaged in reconstructing Iraq after the US-lead invasion. Bechtel manages nuclear dumping and testing sites. Halliburton extracts barite. The Barrick Corporation, which includes members of President Bush's family on its Board of Directors, operates gold mines.

If a native cultural or burial site lies in the way of mining, it will be destroyed. Although Western Shoshone culture and spirituality reside in these sites, Federal agencies are not required to consult with Native Americans before disrupting them. For example, Mount Tenabo, sacred to the Shoshone and the site of burial grounds and cleansing caves, is threatened by the encroachment of gold mines.

Cortez Mining operates a huge facility at the base of the mountain that tears tens of thousands of tons of rock away to produce one ounce of gold. The gold is separated from the rock by a process using cyanide, poisoning the land and surface water. Millions of gallons of water must be pumped from below the water table to the surface. Over time, this water settles back underground, polluted by surface alkaline and chemicals. Besides the violation of their sacred sites, the Danns and other traditional Western Shoshone fear for the poisoning of the land, water and livestock

Yucca Mountain, another sacred site to the Western Shoshone, has been the subject of a decades-long dispute between Native Americans and the US Government. Since the 1950s the US Government has tested hundreds of nuclear weapons on Western Shoshone homelands and disposed of thousands of metric tons of radioactive waste in unlined trenches at the Nevada Test Site. In the late 1970s, the US Defense Department used traditional Shoshone land for the development and testing of the multiple warhead intercontinental ballistic missile, known as the MX.

Currently Congress has passed legislation to dump all of the nuclear industry's high-level nuclear waste at Yucca Mountain. The Bechtel Corporation has been awarded a contract to build and manage this nuclear waste repository, as well as a counter-terrorism training facility where nuclear, biological and chemical weapons are constructed and tested.

Carrie Danns says, "In our traditional way, that our people have told us, the water in the earth's body is like blood in your veins. It's a life system within the earth. And they're taking it out. What's going to happen then? Do you know? Nobody knows".

Western Shoshone Bernice Lalo puts it this way:

> We are who we are because our nation survived here. It is written on our earth. We have arrowheads, burial grounds, sacred sites and all other prehistoric evidence which tells us that we are a sovereign people.... Due to our inherent sovereignty, we as Shoshone people, who still speak our language and have not given up tradition, are obligated to continue it....We are sovereign as our language and culture which are tied to the landmarks of the Shoshone landscape.

* * *

The Danns see the pressure from mining corporations and the Government as the latest wave of "gradual encroachment" that began with the militia incursions of the 1830s. Each wave brings a larger and larger non-traditional presence closer and closer to their homestead.

In the middle of the 19th century, the US Cavalry rode onto Western Shoshone land, killing men, women and children. They brought epidemics of syphilis, tuberculosis and smallpox. The Danns' great-grandparents died of smallpox in the 1850s. Recognizing the danger the disease posed to their communities, many other Shoshone hurled themselves off the cliffs of Mt. Tenabo.

In the 1890s and early 1900s, Dann family children were forced to attend Government schools where their language, culture and religion were, quite literally, beaten out of them. As more white settlers arrived in the area, Shoshone families were pressured to move out. Their crops were burned just before harvest. The US Government began requiring written proof of homestead. Shoshone were prevented from hunting, gathering and wandering.

The history of formal agreements between the US Government and the Western Shoshone begins in 1863, with the Treaty of Ruby Valley. The US recognized the existence and partial sovereignty of the "western Bands" of the Shoshone. The Shoshone agreed that at some point in time they would stop wandering and hunting and settle down on farms and homesteads. The treaty granted white settlers rights to mine and ranch on traditional Shoshone land, and to build railroad and communication lines. It established the right of the Shoshone to compensation for damages to their lands and holdings.

The Department of the Interior is a vast, cabinet-level organ of the US Government charged with the care and use of the land and resources of the United States. One of its many agencies is the Bureau of Land Management (BLM) which oversees land owned or controlled by the Federal Government, about one-eighth of the land in the United States, and manages a wide variety of resources. The Bureau has an enforcement arm—the Rangers—heavily armed federal agents who have the power and profile of military police. The Rangers are equipped and authorized to carry out military-style operations on federal land. In the case of the Danns, the Rangers behave as if there were no dispute, as if they are enforcing the will of the Government, the rightful owner of the land.

The seizure of the Danns' horses and cattle is ostensibly in compensation to the US Government for unpaid fees it charges for grazing on public land. According to the Government, the Danns now owe over three million dollars in fees and fines, an amount no one expects them to be able to pay. According to the Western Shoshone, they are living on their own land, not the Government's.

* * *

In 1934, the US Congress passed the Indian Reorganization Act, which stipulated that federal recognition and support would depend upon the creation of 'tribal' governments based on a model devised by the Secretary of the Interior. Unfamiliar forms of governance were then superimposed on traditional Shoshone decision-making, creating artificial divisions and aggravating existing disputes. As a result the Shoshone nation tended to divide into smaller entities that were less cohesive and more susceptible to outside control.

In 1946 an act of Congress created the Indian Claims Commission (ICC), to investigate suits by Native Americans against the US for illegitimate taking of their land. In 1962, the ICC found against a Shoshone suit, stating,

> The Indian title to the Western Shoshone land was extinguished by the gradual encroachment of settlers and others and by the acquisition, disposition or taking of said lands by the US for its own use and benefit or that of its citizens.

This ICC finding has been criticized by Amnesty International for failing to cite any historical basis for its conclusion.[14]

In 1966, without the participation of the Western Shoshone people, the US arbitrarily set July 1, 1872, as the date of valuation for western Shoshone land, and determined that compensation should be paid for 24 million acres.

In 1979, the US Court of Claims awarded the Western Shoshone (though they did not seek it) $26 million, or $1.08 an acre, an amount determined by the ICC as the 1872 value of the land, without interest. These funds were to be held in trust by the Department of the Interior. Since the Western Shoshone have consistently rejected the money for the last quarter of a century, the fund has grown to $140 million, or about six dollars per acre.

But the value of the land now stands at $250 to $1000 an acre. The value of gold extracted from Western Shoshone land between 1980 and 1997 was $21,539,154,118. Nevada state income from taxes on mine proceeds between 1982 and 1997 was $370,405,000. While the original Western Shoshone land base amounted to over 24 million acres, the land base

---

[14] http://www.amnestyusa.org/justearth/indigenous_people/western_shoshone.html

amounts to less than 27,360 acres, less than 0.1 percent of the original territory.

In 1985 the US Supreme Court handed down its decision in *United States v. Dann*. Western Shoshone territorial title to the land had been terminated by the ICC certification of a monetary "award" in 1979, and that 'payment' had occurred when the Government placed the funds in the Western Shoshone account.

The Danns were prevented from claiming ownership of the land as a defense. The basis of the ruling was that Native Americans are classified as "wards" of the US Government, and so the US could pay itself as "guardian" and hold that the Western Shoshone had been paid.

The fear of traditional Western Shoshone is that if the US manages to distribute any amount of money to even one Shoshone group that will remove the last obstacle to clearing title to the land and granting widespread concessions for private corporate development. Carrie Dann is clear: "The land cannot be sold".

"We have tried to talk reasonably with the Government, but they brush us aside and deal only with those Western Shoshone who agree to be 'good Indians' and take the scraps that are thrown to them", says Dann.

> No money can ever compensate taking the land from our native people. No race of people has ever sold their homeland. Where will our homeland be if we accept the money? Let us walk with dignity and honor and never as a people without a country.

* * *

For more than thirty years the Danns have met this steady erosion of their rights with steadfast individual resistance and wily, determined legal advocacy.

In 1973, Mary Dann was served with her first notice of criminal trespass for walking out on her family's land, just as she had done for seventy years, just as her father had done and just as her grandmother had done. In 1974, the United States Government sued the Danns for trespass, accusing them of grazing cattle on US public land without a permit. The Danns responded that they were using Western Shoshone land in accordance with the Treaty of Ruby Valley.

Once in the spring and again in the autumn of 1992, Bureau of Land Management Rangers conducted forcible round–ups and seizures of the Danns' horses and cattle. Hundreds of head of livestock were taken and sold at drastically low prices to white ranchers.

In the spring seizure, Rangers herded the cattle into a holding corral and prepared to load them onto trucks. But Carrie Dann climbed into the corral and made her way to the middle of the herd, temporarily preventing the loading of the animals. The Rangers were apparently unwilling to risk the trampling of a Native American advocate.

In late 2002, and early 2003, efforts to seize the Danns' livestock intensified. In September of 2002, Rangers and other federal agents rounded up and took away 232 head of cattle. Again the herd was sold at a deep discount; this time, a rancher who knew the Danns bought the bulls and returned them to the sisters.

But nothing the US Government has done to the Danns is as serious — economically and symbolically—as the rounding up and seizure of their horses. Over the course of fifteen days in February of 2003, Bureau of Land Management Rangers forcibly took way 504 horses. Mary and Carrie Dann watched in horror as their half-wild horses became more and more frantic. Helicopters buzzed over horses on the range, forcing them toward corrals. All-terrain vehicles and hired hands herded them into holding pens. The helicopters then gratuitously flew low above the horses, causing them to panic and crash into each other and through corral fencing.

Eventually, the horses were loaded onto trailer trucks and driven away to shelters from which they were dispersed to ranches, farms and horse-care groups. In the course of transport, forty-seven mares and foals died of starvation.

On September 30, 2003, a group of Western Shoshone including the Dann family sued the United States for 60 million acres of land in four states and for compensation for mining on that land. The suit also requests nullification of the 1972 award of $26 million. The suit alleges that the US Government violated the 1863 Treaty of Ruby Valley, contending that while the treaty "expressly recognized permanent Shoshone ownership of the land", most of that land now in fact belongs to the Government. The suit also charges that the Bureau of Indian Affairs "made material representations" to prevent the Western Shoshone from establishing rightful ownership of the land.

In December 2003, the Danns were again served notice of their continued "unauthorized use of federal lands", and ordered to remove their livestock or face further seizures.

* * *

In 1991, to address the violations they were suffering, the Danns founded the Western Shoshone Defense Project (WSDP), an NGO dedicated to protecting, preserving, and restoring traditional lands and rights. Initially a group of volunteer activists focused on the Dann's cause, WSDP has now grown into an established organization with paid staff who advocate and educate on behalf of all Western Shoshone people: their sovereignty, their traditional beliefs, their livelihood, and the environmental sustainability of their lands.

Inspired and encouraged by the Dann sisters, the WSDP has set an example for indigenous groups everywhere in its creative ability to explore and exploit all legal means to defend their cause. They have defended themselves against the US Government with precedent-setting use of regional and international human rights law

The Inter-American Commission on Human Rights (IACHR) is an autonomous entity of the Organization of American States, charged with investigating human rights complaints against governments in the western hemisphere, reporting on human rights conditions in member countries, and fostering adoption of international human rights protections. In 1993, the Indian Law Resource Center filed a petition on behalf of the Danns before the Inter-American Commission on Human Rights. In January of 2003, the Commission found that the Western Shoshone claims of fraud were justified, and that the Bureau of Land Management had violated Western Shoshone rights to due process, to property rights, and to equality under the law.

The report of the IACHR found the Indian Claims Commission in violation on several grounds:

- failure to provide the Danns and the Western Shoshone with due process or to inform them about avenues of redress available to them;
- failure to respect the Danns' right to property and Western Shoshone rights to equal treatment under the law;
- failure to recognize the right of Western Shoshone to negotiate as a nation;
- failure to behave in accordance with international human rights norms.

Furthermore, the IACHR found the United States in violation of international human rights law by virtue of its behavior in land disputes with the Western Shoshone. The Commission found that US claims to Western Shoshone lands are illegal, and that the US had attempted to establish ownership by illegitimate means. The Commission concluded that the US Government must establish a fair legal process to determine the rights of the Danns and other Western Shoshone, and to ensure that US policies regarding property rights of Native Americans comply with the American Declaration on the Rights and Duties of Man. The finding marks the first time the US has been formally sanctioned for its treatment of indigenous peoples within its borders.[15]

In 1999, the UN Committee on the Elimination of All Forms of Racial Discrimination issued an urgent action appeal on behalf of the Western Shoshone. The Committee made a similar statement of concern in 2001.

The same year independent human rights organizations also expressed concern: "Amnesty International is concerned about the alleged violations against [the Danns], in particular their rights to equality under the law, to be free of discrimination, to fair trial and to property".

The Western Shoshone Defense Project contends that United States Government behavior towards the Western Shoshone violates its obligations as a state party to the Convention on Elimination of All Forms of Racial Discrimination, the American Declaration on the Rights and Duties of Man, and the International Covenant on Civil and Political Rights. Specific rights being violated that are guaranteed in these documents include: the right to

---

[15] http://www.amnestyusa.org/justearth/indigenous_people/united_states.pdf

property; the right to equality before the law; the right to due process; the right to cultural identity; and the right to self-determination. Moreover, US treatment of Western Shoshone land rights and due process access compares unfavorably with the treatment accorded similar rights of non-indigenous people.

Native Americans have increasingly presented information on human rights violations to the UN Working Group on Indigenous Populations. They have been involved in writing the UN Draft Declaration on the Rights of Indigenous Peoples, and the Draft American Declaration on the Rights of Indigenous Peoples. Native Americans have testified before the UN Human Rights Commission, the UN Committee on Elimination of Racial Discrimination and the Inter-American Commission on Human Rights. All these bodies have issued reports and findings critical of US law and practice regarding Native Americans.

The UN has created a Permanent Forum on Indigenous Issues, through which native people can bring abuses to world attention. The UN Convention Concerning Indigenous and Tribal Peoples in Independent Countries, is the only international treaty dealing solely with native people. The Convention provides protections for indigenous lands, health, education and employment. The US has not ratified the Convention.

Julie Fishel of the Western Shoshone Defense Project argues that the treatment of the Danns and other Shoshone prevents the US Government from securing the trust of indigenous peoples anywhere in the world. The US denies itself the moral authority it might need to intervene on behalf of indigenous people whose rights are being violated, especially in Central America. Moreover, Project members are concerned that if the traditional Western Shoshone do not prevail in their struggle, repressive forces in other countries will be encouraged to violate the rights of indigenous peoples.

On November 17, 2003, US Congressional Representative Raul Grijalva, a Democrat from Arizona, wrote to Gale Norton, Secretary of the Department of the Interior, calling for an explanation of the legal rationale for taking title to Western Shoshone land, a justification for recent treatment of Western Shoshone homesteads and an accounting of contacts the Government has had with corporations interested in developing Shoshone land. Congressman Grijalva wrote in the context of a debate over legislation known as The

Western Shoshone Distribution Bill, which would force the award of $145 million to the Western Shoshone. In his letter, Grijalva questioned how the US could have ended Native American ownership of the land, saying, "Gradual encroachment is not a legally valid method of taking or extinguishing title, and the Western Shoshone have never sold, ceded or in any manner transferred title".

The United Nations Declaration on Human Rights Defenders states in Article 9 that "in the exercise of human rights and fundamental freedoms..., everyone has the right, individually and in association with others, to benefit from an effective remedy and to be protected in the event of the violation of those rights".

* * *

Carrie and Mary Dann recognize that they may not live to see US history 'corrected', and recognition and respect for Shoshone achievements, philosophy, spirituality and land. However, through the Western Shoshone Defense Project and its persistence in claiming international human rights standards for the Western Shoshone people, they will leave a legacy of courage and advocacy for indigenous activists.

When asked what her goals are, Carrie replies, "The truth to be told and leave me alone".

Jeff Dietrich
Los Angeles, California

"Going to jail is part of the witness" — Jeff Dietrich

On March 15, 2003, Robert Jefferson (Jeff) Dietrich was arraigned and charged with trespass for sprinkling holy water and praying the Rosary on the steps of the United States federal office building in Los Angeles. He was tried and sentenced to fifty days in the LA Metropolitan Detention Center.

For over thirty years, Jeff Dietrich has lived a life of service as a member of the Catholic Worker community in Los Angeles. Dietrich's life and work represent a commitment to serving the poor, a responsibility required by both his faith and by Scripture.

In these thirty years Dietrich has been arrested more than thirty times for non-violent protests for the rights of homeless people and against the development of increasingly lethal military weapons.

He has served prison sentences ranging from ten days to six months. He was held in solitary confinement for three weeks. His health has been compromised by inadequate prison medical treatment. He was placed in US federal prisons where he was the only inmate charged with a political offense. Dietrich's wife, Catherine Morris, has also served time in jail for protesting the US war in Iraq.

The charges against him and the prison terms he has served act as a warning to other human rights defenders that peaceful protest in the USA may well have grave consequences.[16]

* * *

Robert Jefferson Dietrich grew up in Fullerton, east of Los Angeles in Orange County. He was raised as a conventional Roman Catholic whose family prayed and attended church. However, although the element of

---

[16] Unless otherwise cited, information on Jeff Dietrich is derived from interviews conducted with Dietrich in 2003.

service to others was not emphasized, that message lodged in Dietrich. As he says, "Caring for the poor is crucial to our own salvation".

He attended Catholic secondary school in nearby Santa Ana, and went on to the California State University at Fullerton. Like many of his contemporaries, Dietrich experienced a crisis of conscience over the US war in Southeast Asia. Upon graduation, he received a draft notice requiring him to join the armed forces. He refused induction, saying, "It's not that I don't want to serve, it's that I don't want to serve in the way this country wants me to serve. I want to serve life, not death". Dietrich decided to spend the time until his probable arrest by traveling for six months in Europe. He fully expected to be taken into custody when he returned, but a warrant was apparently never issued.

While making his way back to California, he met a group of people involved with the Catholic Worker community. As he learned about what they were doing he says, "It occurred to me that this is what Christ would be doing – clothing the naked, sheltering the homeless, and burning draft files".

Soon afterward Dietrich met and married Catherine Morris; service to the poor was part of their marriage vows.

* * *

During his years as Governor of California in the 1970s, Ronald Regan drastically cut social services, forcing the closing of many residential mental health facilities, federally subsidized housing units, and job training programs. One cumulative result has been a steady population of 8,000 poor people living in cheap hotels or abandoned buildings in downtown Los Angeles, and an additional 3000 living on the street. This is where the city's most unsightly problems get dumped. As Dietrich says, "This is the tail end of the whole system".[17]

In response to this crisis, the Catholic Worker community in Los Angeles runs a soup kitchen and medical clinic offering free food and health care to downtown LA's destitute and homeless. In 1994 the Catholic Worker forced the city to install portable toilets for the homeless, but not until after they

---

[17] Ben Ehrenreich, 'Off My Back', *Los Angeles Weekly*, 18 May 2001.

had protested by blocking the entrance to the men's room at City Hall. In 1998, however, many of these toilets were removed because of a budget cutback. In response Catholic Worker members staged a sit-in at the office of Mayor Richard Riordan, where they sang hymns and held signs reading, "Outhouses for People Without Houses". The media loved it. The toilets were back on the street by 5 *p.m.* the same day.

The community also protects the homeless on LA's inner city from the private security forces, hired by downtown businesses, known as the "Shirts" because of their color-coded uniform blouses. Although without the legal authority of police officers, the "Shirts" routinely behave as if they were official. Their job is to remove anything unsightly that would deter paying customers from the downtown business district. "Anything unsightly" includes the homeless. The garment district's Yellow Shirts set the precedent in 1995 when they drove the homeless out of their territory, sometimes "escorting" them to the district boundary.

The "Shirts" systematically confiscate the shopping carts the homeless use to move or store their possessions. They further harass the homeless in a variety of other ways. They prevent street people from picking through trash to find containers to recycle for cash. They often call in the police to issue tickets for violations such as vagrancy or jaywalking. When a few unpaid tickets accrue, the consequence is jail time.[18]

The issue is not simply bullying and criminalizing of the homeless or denying them basic services and facilities. More significant is the increasing privatization of public space and of law enforcement. City authorities have encouraged this trend: every service the businesses pay for themselves means one less expense for the city. Dietrich puts it this way:

> From our perspective, the shirts are a private army. They're no different from a vigilante group formed and paid for by business people and property owners....They want no experiences that diminish people's desire to spend money.

The American Civil Liberties Union has charged that business district interests have produced a private police force engaged in "a crude campaign

---

[18] Ehrenreich.

of intimidation.... to run the homeless out of certain sections of the city forever".[19]

In June of 1999 the Catholic Worker began buying and distributing new shopping carts to the homeless. These carts were painted black and came with a certificate asserting that they belonged to the Catholic Worker but could be used by any homeless person. They bear a sign that says, "Unauthorized possession of this cart by non-homeless persons is a violation of state law". Dietrich said at the time, "Our carts have become a precious commodity as it has become clear that the police will not take them".[20]

Asked why he has spent so much time and effort on shopping carts, Dietrich replies:

> It is the shopping cart that allows the homeless person to maintain the last shred of human dignity. Nothing symbolizes more graphically the desperation and degradation of homeless poverty than a shopping cart. To give a shopping cart to a homeless person is an act of complicity and codependency, if not outright criminal conspiracy. But it is unconscionable for any social service agency to continue fostering the illusion that it is still possible to aspire to the American dream. Over the past several decades, our nation has consistently eliminated the lifelines, stepladders and safety nets that historically made it possible for the poor in a complex industrial society to transition out of poverty....we have virtually slammed the door on the poor, creating a permanent homeless underclass. The real purpose of our free shopping carts is not simply to help the poor or keep them out of jail, though it is definitely that. The real purpose is to ensure that the poor, with the rolling emblem of their poverty and suffering, will not be entirely invisible to the community.[21]

When the Roman Catholic Cardinal Roger Mahoney of Los Angeles decided to spend $50 million on a new cathedral in one of the poorest areas of the

---

[19] Press release, American Civil Liberties Union, April 2001.

[20] Arizona State University Press, July 1999.

[21] Jeff Dietrich, 'A Rolling Symbol of Society's Heartlessness', *Los Angeles Times*, 4 August 1998.

city, Dietrich and his colleagues scaled the wall of the old cathedral, sat on top of the bell tower 200 feet above the ground, and unfurled an enormous banner that read, "We reclaim the church for the poor". Dietrich recalls,

> When the police finally came, they yelled up to us, 'Be sensible. Come down from there and talk to us'. If we were sensible we never would have scaled the walls of an old abandoned cathedral and climbed into an open window and scrambled up the rickety stairs of the dilapidated bell tower in the first place. If we were sensible we wouldn't be sitting 200 feet above the ground on top of an earthquake damaged structure....Only devious criminals or obstreperous schoolboys do such things. Sensible people obey the law and mind their own business.[22]

Dietrich spoke at the time,

> Thus we take our stand with Francis of Assisi, who answered God's call to rebuild the church with a life of poverty and service. And in this century we stand with Oscar Romero, the martyred archbishop of El Salvador, when he said, 'The temple shall remain unfinished until all are housed in dignity'.

Later that year, Dietrich and others temporarily stopped the groundbreaking for the new Cathedral. They sat on an earthmover, held rosaries, and chanted Hail Mary's. They held a banner that read, "Let the Cathedral stand unfinished until ALL are housed in dignity". The protesters announced that they would leave if Cardinal Mahoney would build a mission for the poor instead of a cathedral. They were arrested and charged with trespass. Said Dietrich, "From the Tower of Babel to the pyramids of Egypt, Scripture has been skeptical of large-scale building projects, recognizing that grand buildings and great edifices go hand-in-hand with great wealth and political oppression".

Controversy has since arisen over the high price of being interred within the cathedral. There are 1300 crypts and 5000 niches; prices for a crypt will start at $50,000. This means that the cathedral, like so much else in LA, will be

---

[22] Jeff Dietrich, 'The Great Cathedral Caper', *Los Angeles Lay Catholic Mission*, January 2002.

largely reserved for the rich and famous. Presumably there will be room for the major donors to the building fund, people such as Sir Daniel Donohue (a $25 million contributor), Rupert Murdoch ($10 million), Roy Disney and Bob Hope. [23]

Of the connection between serving the poor and opposing the construction of a new cathedral, Dietrich says,

> The poor you will always have with you and they are often a pain in the neck. But without the poor there is no cross, there is no resurrection, there is no Easter. The cost of the new cathedral soars from a promised cap of $45 million to a new high of $163 million. The poor you will always have with you, but when it comes to building cathedrals they are a pain in the neck. [24]

* * *

Most of Dietrich's arrests have been in consequence of his protest against US wars and the production of the machines of war.

His first arrest in 1979 came as a result of a non-violent protest against US armament sales. Dietrich received a six-month sentence, which he felt was excessive and unjust. As Dietrich puts it, "They're giving me six months in jail for things that most people get a fifty-dollar fine. Were it not for the political nature of the acts, I would not be getting so much time".

In June of 2000, Dietrich entered Vandenberg Air Force Base near Lompoc, California, to protest the renewed development of the "Star Wars" missile defense shield.

At Vandenburg, counter-insurgency satellites are launched and elements of the National Missile Defense (NMD) are tested. Deployment of the NMD constituted a violation of the 1972 Anti-Ballistic Missile Treaty with Russia, and led to the voiding of the treaty. The 30th Space Wing at Vandenberg is the Air Force Space Command unit responsible for all Department of

---

[23] Larry B. Stammer, 'Mother Church of a Secular City?' *Los Angeles Times*, 25 August 2002.

[24] Jeff Dietrich, 'Perspective on Easter?' *Los Angeles Times*, 4 April 1998.

Defense space and missile launch activities on the West Coast and all US satellites destined for polar orbit. The Space Wing contributes to the development of all intercontinental ballistic missiles and supports West Coast launch activities for the Air Force, Department of Defense, National Aeronautics and Space Administration, and various private industry contractors.

When Dietrich pled guilty, the prosecutor recommended a sentence of time served and five years probation. Dietrich rejected the proposal, stating that he could not honestly promise to comply with the conditions of the probation since he intended to continue to oppose missile testing at Vandenburg.

Dietrich refused a jury trial and chose to defend himself, saying,

> I pled proudly guilty. I indisputably committed the action, but I was proudly guilty of doing it.... I could not in conscience cooperate with the punishment. If the judge wishes to impose a punishment on me, then I don't have any choice in that. I'm certainly not going to make a choice to pay a fine, or come to see a probation officer, or to promise not to go back to Vandenburg; that requires my cooperation in my own punishment, and that would say that the state had some right in punishing me and I don't believe that. I believe that what I did is the right thing to do.

On Good Friday 2001, Dietrich and other Catholic Worker members conducted a "Stations of the Cross" demonstration in El Segundo, California, a part of Los Angeles County that is home to many major US military contractors. In a march intended to reflect Christ's agony, the protesters began in front of the Raytheon Corporation, moved on to Hughes Aircraft, then to Boeing and other defense suppliers. At the time, Dietrich declared, "We want to focus attention on the fact that the poor are being crucified on Bush's military budget". Dietrich noted that the $40 billion earmarked for development of the "Star Wars" system in 2001, was almost equal to the country's health and human services budget.

In 2003 during the buildup for war in Iraq Dietrich was arrested on six separate occasions for demonstrating against the war: on January 1 at the Tournament of Roses Parade in Pasadena; four times between January 1 and March 12, 2003, at the US federal building in Los Angeles; and once at the Raytheon Corporation.

The New Year's Day Rose Parade is an enormous event that draws hundreds of thousands of live spectators every year and is broadcast on national television. Dietrich was arrested for standing before the lead vehicles and temporarily delaying the start of the parade.

At the LA Federal Building, Dietrich was arrested for: praying on the steps; blocking the sidewalk; and entering the building without permission.

At Raytheon, Dietrich was arrested for "impeding traffic". Raytheon produces, among many other things, the Tomahawk Cruise Missile, the HAWK Air Defense Missile, the Sidewinder missile, the HARM Targeting System, the Space Tracking and Surveillance System, and the Universal Automatic Identification System.

After his Raytheon arrest, the prosecutor assigned to his case recognized his name from previous arrests. Dietrich was then charged with trespass and refusal to disperse. He was held for two months without a sentence at the Metropolitan Detention Center in downtown Los Angeles, and only released on the day after President Bush declared that victory in Iraq had been achieved.

* * *

Many of Dietrich's fellow activists try to make a political or moral point by using international law to fight the charges against them. Dietrich supports such efforts, but tries to make a similar point by *not* contesting the charges against him. He believes that part of Christian witness involves, "standing up and taking responsibility for what you are doing. Going to jail is part of the witness".

Dietrich describes the process of being charged, held, judged, sentenced and imprisoned this way:

It's humiliating personally, but from the perspective of Christian resistance, it's important to stand up for what you believe....We believe we are following in the footsteps of Christ. The humiliation we endure brings us closer to the experience of the cross.

At Kern County Jail, Dietrich found himself the only prisoner charged with a political crime. He became concerned for the other inmates, most of whom were being held for violation of immigration regulations. He learned that many were facing eight or ten year sentences for their second or third attempts to cross the border with Mexico. He noted that the process of charging and sentencing these inmates moved excruciatingly slowly. Immigrants often spend months, sometimes years, in prison before their cases are finally resolved. Because they are from other countries, they are unable to post bail.

Dietrich spent the last two months of this sentence at Metropolitan Detention Center in Los Angeles. As an act of conscience, he refused to work to support the prison. As a result, he was placed in solitary confinement – twenty-four-hour lock-up in one cell without sunlight – for three weeks.

Dietrich felt that prison authorities went out of their way to make his experience as humiliating and demeaning as possible. He says he was treated not so much as an animal, but more as an object. He was stripped and subjected to a body-cavity search before he could receive any visitors. He developed a severe staphylococcus infection that became even more serious when he did not receive adequate medical attention. Since Dietrich's release, Kern County Jail, as a result of its inability to improve its treatment of prisoners, has lost its contract to hold federal prisoners.

* * *

Dietrich's activities are almost certainly monitored by local, state, and federal law enforcement agencies. Over the course of the war in Iraq, rights advocates have accused the Bush Administration of seeking to limit freedom of speech and assembly for anti-war demonstrators. Opponents of US policy in Iraq have sued the Government to discover why they were placed on a 'no fly' list intended to prevent terrorists from boarding planes. Activists have charged that law enforcement officials had infiltrated demonstration planning meetings and spied on antiwar rallies.

Rights advocates and legal scholars have expressed their fear that the Federal Bureau of Investigation (FBI) intelligence activities could mean a return to the abuses of the 1960s and 1970s when former FBI Director J. Edgar Hoover used the FBI for mass spying on political protesters and civil rights activists. Anthony Romero, Executive Director of the American Civil Liberties Union said, "The FBI is dangerously targeting Americans who are engaged in nothing more than lawful protest and dissent....What the FBI regards as potential terrorism strikes me as civil disobedience". Herman Schwartz, a professor of Constitutional law at American University said,

> As a matter of principle, this has a very chilling effect on peaceful demonstration. If you go around telling people, 'We're going to ferret out information on demonstrators', that deters people. People don't want their names and pictures in FBI files.[25]

Hoover-era abuses included the Cointelpro program aimed at harassing and stigmatizing perceived political enemies. Those excesses led to legislative and administrative restrictions on the FBI's political investigations. The restrictions were relaxed in 2002, however, when US Attorney General John Ashcroft gave FBI agents the charge to attend any event "open to the public", including political rallies and mosques.[26]

On November 23, 2003, the *New York Times* reported on a confidential FBI memorandum in which the agency said it had, "collected extensive information on the tactics, training, and organization of anti-war demonstrators and has advised local law enforcement officials to report any suspicious activity at protests to its counterterrorism squads".[27]

* * *

---

[25] Eric Lichtblau, *New York Times*, 23 November 2003.

[26] Ibid.

[27] Ibid.

Dietrich is part of a growing phenomenon in the USA: local human rights activists and advocates who feel that they must work locally to improve the lives of the people in their communities, but also feel they must respond to the abuses committed worldwide by their national government. The bridge between these two commitments is often formed by the ethic, the spirit, and the language of human rights. Community activist leaders in the USA increasingly identify each other as human rights advocates, activists who may never travel to a designated international human rights conference in Brussels or Beijing or Buenos Aires, but who nonetheless are beginning to see themselves as part of a worldwide movement to redress centuries of inequity. Dietrich's central commitment is to protecting and restoring human rights: the rights of the poor in the US; the rights of those throughout the world who will be violated by US arms and weapons systems; the rights of local activists and advocates to design, build and maintain a community of care.

Homelessness, war, and a 200 million dollar cathedral: the connection lies in the commitment of the US Government and the private sector to allocating the nation's resources to the perpetuation of armaments, business interests, and the wealthy at the expense of the poor, the disabled, and the needy. And it lies in the commitment of Jeff Dietrich and his colleagues to change all that. He believes that all the homeless could be housed in comfort and all the hungry fed full for the cost of one weapon system. He sees that placing such a high economic and political priority on ever-increasing military spending prevents the United States from approaching its potential in education, health care, and human services.

The United Nations Declaration on Human Rights Defenders recognizes "the relationship between international peace and security and the enjoyment of human rights and fundamental freedoms". Article 5 of the Declaration states that

> for the purpose of promoting and protecting human rights and fundamental freedoms, everyone has the right, individually and in association with others, at the national and international levels... to meet or assemble peacefully.

Article 6 of the Declaration states that "everyone has the right, individually and in association with others...freely to publish, impart or disseminate to others views, information and knowledge on all human rights and fundamental freedoms".

Jeff Dietrich describes his way of living as a paradox. On one hand, living outside the boundaries of the conventional society is a risk and a sacrifice: low pay, no insurance or retirement benefits, no social security. But, he says, living a life of service in a community of solidarity with the poor offers a singular form of freedom, freedom from the burden of consumerism, from the limitations of conformity, from unwitting support of inequality and violence. In his words,

> The conventional culture is antithetical to the Gospel. To live the life of the Gospel, of witness, you must live an alternative life....The community and the service are all of a piece. We're about justice – restoring to the poor the money that has been stolen from them. I feel good about what I do. If I die tomorrow I feel my life will have been worthwhile.

Brenda and Wanda Henson
Ovett, Mississippi

"We do not seek tolerance and acceptance. We seek freedom from oppression, intimidation and harassment. We seek justice and a legal system that is capable and willing to defend our rights" – Brenda and Wanda Henson

Brenda and Wanda Henson are a lesbian couple living in the rural hamlet of Ovett, Mississippi. For nearly twenty-five years they have advocated for activists who provide food and clothing to poor communities. For over twenty years they have protected women seeking rightful custody of their children. For fifteen years they have been leaders of the struggle for lesbian and women's rights in Mississippi and the South.

But over the same years, the Hensons have documented over 100 hate crimes committed against them because of their advocacy. They have been shot at and run off the road. They've received bomb threats, hate mail, and harassing phone calls. They've been refused service by local businesses and had their checks returned with Bible verses scrawled on them. They found their dog hanging from the mailbox.

Despite these ordeals, which continue to the present day, the Hensons have never wavered in their commitment to advocacy and activism. As Wanda Henson says, "In the face of terror we have managed to survive".[28]

* * *

Brenda Henson was born in Dayton, Ohio, in 1945. Her father abused his wife and his children. Brenda dropped out of high school in the ninth grade and gave birth to her first child at 16.

In her teenage years she began providing access to food for people in need: transporting people to food banks, collecting food, and helping poor people get food stamps. She dates the emergence of her political and human rights

---

[28] Unless otherwise cited, information on Brenda and Wanda Henson is derived from interviews conducted with the Hensons in late 2003 and early 2004.

consciousness from the racial demonstrations and riots of the late 1960s, particularly in nearby Cincinnati.

In the late 1970s she lived in Tallahassee, Florida, where she worked for the abolition of the death penalty in that state, which is second only to Texas in its number of executions. Married to an abusive husband, she finally "ran for her life" and settled in Gulfport, Mississippi, where she found work at a reproductive health clinic. She has vivid memories of a flatbed truck parked in front of the clinic from which the mayor and church groups, accompanied by a band, would denounce pregnancy counseling. She remembers escorting teenage girls through a gauntlet of local women, some grabbing at the girls to prevent them from entering the clinic.

In the 1980s she recaptured her education, passing a high school equivalency course and examination. She graduated from the University of Southern Mississippi, went on to earn a Master's degree in education, and is currently working on a doctoral dissertation.

Wanda Henson was born and raised in Pascagoula, Mississippi, a racially charged region where her white community taught her that African Americans had no souls and that their brains were in their heels so that if you kicked them hard enough there you could kill them.

She graduated from high school in 1972. Like Brenda, she married an abusive husband at 16 and had two children. In 1975 Wanda came out as a lesbian and was divorced. Two years later her former husband and his new wife took the children for a holiday visit and never brought them back. Although Wanda was working as a nurse, owned her own home, and taught Sunday school, a court awarded custody of the children to the father because Wanda was a lesbian. Four years later the children ran away from him, and Wanda regained custody.

In 1981 Brenda and Wanda met at the women's clinic in Gulfport and soon began living together.

* * *

From then on, the Hensons have worked together on a widening range of social justice issues.

In 1982 they began advocating for women involved in custody disputes. They made it possible for many mothers to take their cases out of Mississippi to courts in more progressive states.

In 1987 the Hensons opened Southern Wild Sisters Unlimited, a community bookstore providing resources and advocacy on gay and lesbian concerns, HIV treatment, and sexual abuse. People in need who could not qualify for government-funded social services were often referred to the Hensons.

The bookstore became a flashpoint for hostility against the Hensons and their lifestyle. When they painted the exterior trim of the bookstore a shade of lavender, they provoked the ire of the local real estate appraiser. Vandals repeatedly stole the store's disabled parking sign. Their electricity was disrupted, preventing them from opening on time. They received numerous warnings that the store would be closed down. Rumors circulated that they were witches. The store was broken into and robbed. Church members came to the store to buy books so they could teach children "what sin is". One such customer said to Brenda, "I need to tell you something. People are talking about burning your place down". When Brenda asked why, the customer said, "Because you're Satanists and lesbians". To which Brenda could only reply, "We're not Satanists".

A private investigator and an agent from the Federal Bureau of Investigation (FBI) questioned the Hensons on the whereabouts of children involved in custody disputes. The Hensons were the subjects of investigations into what national groups they represented, because in Mississippi being identified with an "outside group" is to be discredited. The local newspaper ran an editorial suggesting that if the Hensons wanted to be terrorists they "should go live with Qadhafi". Brenda says of this period, "It's not that you're confronted with violence every day. It's that you face the potential for violence every day".

In 1989 the Hensons established Sister Spirit, a non-profit service and advocacy organization addressing twenty-one specific concerns that had been raised during their time at the bookstore. The Hensons' commitment to holistic advocacy is reflected in the mission statement of Sister Spirit, which sets out a mandate:

To make available information, referral, education, advocacy, and meeting space to address social issues including, but not limited to, racism, sexism, homophobia, ageism, lookism, fat oppression, anti-Semitism, family abuse and violence, sexual abuse and incest, housing, hunger, health care, fair labor practices, environmental issues and much more.

In 1990 they created the Gulf Coast Women's Festival, an annual weekend event of education and inspiration for feminists and lesbians. The following year, however, local authorities in Gulfport refused to provide space for their festival. In response, the Hensons purchased 120 acres of isolated forest land in Ovett, Mississippi, and established Camp Sister Spirit. They moved to Ovett, initially intending to reduce their activist time as both Brenda and Wanda were working on doctorate degrees at the University of Southern Mississippi. Nevertheless they continued to tend to the food bank in Gulfport, at that point serving seventy families.

* * *

Ovett is an unincorporated village in southeast Mississippi, a region of cotton and corn, cattle and poultry, three hours from New Orleans. Ovett offers a general store, a gas station, and an auto parts store. The Hensons also found prejudice, ignorance, fear, and violence there.

Rickey Cole, the head of the Democratic Party of Jones County, where Ovett is located, articulated a common concern. He said he was afraid for his pregnant sister to drive by the Henson home because like witches they might "mark the fetus". Townspeople expressed the fear that the Hensons would steal little girls and teach local women how to be lesbians. There was concern that the Hensons would attract gay men, who would contaminate the water supply with AIDS. Brenda said, "The local shopkeepers won't sell to us, or they charge us two or three times the going rate for something".

Partly in response to the presence of the Hensons, a local militia group was formed. Their newsletter, "The Revolutionary", fabricated a story about a missing 13-year-old girl being held against her will at Camp Sister Spirit. Militia members put up a sign near Camp Sister Spirit that read, "The Spirit of America is Going Strong — Any Other Spirit Don't Belong". At the University of Southern Mississippi the Hensons were approached by a young woman who, apparently fearing for her husband's wellbeing, warned that he and other men were planning to kill them.

One of the volunteers at Camp Sister Spirit said, "The same tactics that locals were using against African Americans in the sixties, they're using against us. I've tried for over a year to get someone with some heavy equipment to help us rebuild these roads in here. Every time I find somebody, somehow, somebody from Ovett finds out who they are and they threaten to burn their equipment or hurt them. We had a local man up the road who we were buying hay from for a while. Two of his calves were shot and he was told by one of our neighbors not to do business with us any more".[29]

The atmosphere of threat and violence was compressed into one horrific moment on the morning of November 8, 1993. That was the day Brenda's daughter stepped out onto the porch and found their dog killed and hung from the mailbox. Sanitary napkins had been stuffed into the mailbox and a bullet fired through it.

The next month 250 people came to a meeting at the Ovett Community Center to discuss methods of getting rid of the Hensons. Public officials, including the Democratic Congressman for the district and the attorney for the county Board of Supervisors, promised to apply state laws prohibiting sodomy against the Hensons.[30]

A month later, in January of 1994, John Allen, a Baptist pastor, and John Hendry, the local head of Mississippi Family Values, held a meeting to raise money for a lawsuit against Camp Sister Spirit. In a town of 400 souls, 350 attended the meeting. Allen accused the Hensons of having a "radical agenda". Many people at the meeting said they feared that the camp would become a "hub of homosexual activity". Hendry wrote in a local newspaper:

> I am personally not ready to have south Mississippi turned into
> a haven for every stray lesbian that wants to settle down in

---

[29] Jeff Harmon, 'The Sisters Take on the Rednecks', *New Statesman*, 28 August 1998.

[30] Press release, National Gay and Lesbian Task Force, 8 December 1993.

Jones County! ... I hope together we can find some logical, legal solution to rid our county of this blight on our land.[31]

The lawsuit was intended to forestall intervention by the Federal Government, which had taken an interest in the dispute. Allen and Hendry also sought damages of $50,000 each. A frustrated Brenda Henson said at the time, "They're showing by the suit that they really don't want to resolve this. They don't want to solve the problem; they want to make an issue. All we want to do is live in peace". Brenda added, "This is a case of men in suits stirring up the fears of men in overalls".

Brenda recalls that a local man told a visiting lesbian film-maker that if the Hensons won the lawsuit, "I'd really hate to see all those buildings burned down and corpses stacked up ... I'll do whatever I have to do to protect my family".[32]

Allen and Hendry's suit stated,

> The question is the reasonableness or unreasonableness of conducting an educational and cultural retreat center, which is to be the battleground for the gay rights movement in America, in the midst of an essentially residential community ... Put a slightly different way, a nuisance may be merely a right thing in the wrong place—like a pig in the parlor instead of the barnyard... Camp Sister Spirit is simply a case of the pig in the parlor.

In July of 1995 the suit was dismissed, but the court stated that the "fears and concerns of the plaintiffs are genuine and are justified under the evidence".[33]

During this period the Hensons had regular contact with only one neighbor—and he wasn't happy about it. He owned land to the north and south of the Hensons' property and intended to hunt through their 120 acres. Wanda Henson recalls,

---

[31] 'Camp Sister Spirit', Associated Press, 7 March 1994.
[32] Ibid.
[33] Harmon.

When we told him that our land was a wildlife refuge and would never be hunted again, he was enraged. He told us that we had no right; considering himself the patriarch of this community, he thought he could run us off. So far he has failed. People from around the country have stuck with us.

The Hensons' water pipes run through their neighbor's land. One month they received a bill for 187,000 gallons of water. The neighbor has made it clear that to get access to the pipes the Hensons would have to take him to court.

The Hensons experienced more frightening threats and harassment. Dead animals were left at the camp, including a poisonous copperhead snake. They endured comments from townspeople such as "Stay with your own kind you pervert" and "We were here first and we don't need you here". A car was set on fire in the Hensons' driveway and burned the front of their property. Local police reported it as an accident.

Brenda recalls the time she was pursued by a group of men in a truck.

They chased me home and tried to run me off the road....I jumped in my truck and was going as fast as I could go. Wanda was back at the camp listening to me scream on her two-way radio and she was going crazy. We don't necessarily like guns but we had purchased them. We were going to be pacifists but not stupid pacifists. She picked up the 30-30 and just as I came in on two wheels, Wanda was running down the hill and the guys saw her and took off. It was so scary for me. I really got the sense I could die.

During 1993 and 1994, the attacks on the Hensons drew national attention. In November of 1993, reporters from around the country set up camp in Ovett. The Hensons appeared on Oprah Winfrey's widely watched television program, the television news magazine *20/20*, and CNN's interview program *Larry King Live*. Their struggle was featured in national news media, and they made speaking tours throughout the USA. The coverage was largely sympathetic, although conservative columnist and former presidential candidate Pat Buchanan referred to the Hensons as "nature-worshipping

64

jezebels". It was during this period that the Hensons became recognized nationwide as advocates for the rights of lesbians and feminists.[34]

The Federal Government also took notice. US Attorney General Janet Reno ordered the Community Relations Service of the Department of Justice to intervene and mediate. This was the first time such action had been taken in a civil rights case based on sexual identity. Reno also ordered the FBI to investigate threatening letters mailed to the Hensons, a federal offense. Reno wrote to the National Gay and Lesbian Task Force saying, "The intolerance and bigotry demonstrated by some of the people of Ovett have no place in this country". The mediation, however, failed. The atmosphere of violence remained. The threats continued.[35]

During 1994 the Ovett school bus driver would slow down as he passed the Hensons' home and sound his horn to signal the children on board to start screaming, "Faggots!" Several times men appeared on their land, some intoxicated, some with guns, some both. On one occasion four men and three boys gained entry to Camp Sister Spirit. One of the boys appeared in "skinhead" style with a shaved head, combat boots, and military fatigues. On two separate occasions an intoxicated man in a jeep rammed through the front gate of the camp. In the autumn of 1994, a supporter's house was burned down. A caller threatened, "Expect the KKK to burn a cross on you".

But the Hensons' advocacy also continued. Camp Sister Spirit became a nationally recognized source of feminist and lesbian training, motivation, resources, and respite. It provides a food bank, counseling on coming out, and speakers for universities. Author and feminist Phyllis Chesler says,

> Camp Sister Spirit is like Woodstock, Lesbian Nation, and the Michigan Women's Music Festival, but it's also like Mississippi Freedom Summer, the Mothers of the Plaza de Mayo, a Goddess Grove, and a Girl Scout Camp.[36]

The Hensons also continued their work at the Gulfport food bank, which had grown from 70 to 300 families as a result of their television exposure. They

---

[34] Victoria Scanlan Stefanakos, 'Firsthand Hate', *The Advocate*, 19 January 1999.
[35] Ibid.
[36] Phyllis Chesler, 'Sister, Fear Has No Place Here', *On the Issues*, Fall 1994.

also extended the kinds of assistance provided, helping with housing and employment. Brenda says, "We were moving people from subsistence and isolation to buying their own homes and establishing a community".

But their notoriety also attracted the attention and interference of officials at the state capital in Jackson. The Hensons were harassed by government agents and warned that they could not use food distribution to "further their cause". As a result the food bank was forced to close in 1996 although the Hensons continue to provide services on an emergency basis.

In the late 1990s the Hensons began working with advocates in other areas of concern. They received the support of national civil rights leader Ben Chaney. They provided assistance to the families of victims of "jailhouse suicide", young African American men hanged while in police or prison custody. They brought diverse organizations and individual advocates together to learn how to address racism and homophobia.

In 2000, the Hensons were invited to Northern Ireland to speak at the University of Ulster and meet with members of the National Assembly. They made comments on the Good Friday agreement, which included provisions on sexual identity rights. Brenda has written that Lower Ormeau Road in Belfast felt like Ovett: "The eyes of those we met while walking along the Lower Ormeau were alert, not ever looking you directly in the eye and watching every car that passed".

* * *

Author Phyllis Chesler says,

> It's hard to remain radical in feminist terms when your sexual [identity] is feared and hated….It's hard to remain 'in service' to others when you yourself remain unsafe at every moment. That's why what Brenda and Wanda Henson are doing at Camp Sister Spirit….is so important. The Hensons have not dropped out — nor have they sold out.[37]

---

[37] Chesler.

Camp Sister Spirit is expanding its land holdings in Ovett. The Hensons host a statewide summit meeting and training for lesbian, gay, bisexual and transgender activists. Their annual festival now offers legal and financial advice as well as training and motivation for girls and young women. More than 4,000 visitors and volunteers from eleven different countries have been at the camp.[38]

As they have for the last fourteen years, the Hensons continue to provide clothing and medical supplies to a mission they established in Isla Mujeres, Mexico. Their US advocacy is known even there where one woman said to them, "Please don't let the gringoes kill you".

The United Nations Declaration on Human Rights Defenders states in Article 12 that "everyone has the right, individually and in association with others, to participate in peaceful activities against violations of human rights and fundamental freedoms;" and,

> The State shall take all necessary measures to ensure the protection by the competent authorities of everyone, individually and in association with others, against any violence, threats, retaliation, *de facto* or *de jure* adverse discrimination, pressure or any other arbitrary action as a consequence of his or her legitimate exercise of the rights referred to in the present Declaration.

Lately, the Hensons have returned to the kind of work they pursued in Gulfport. Wanda is a nurse practitioner in Centreville, Mississippi, at a facility started in 1929 to provide health care for African Americans. Wanda ministers to the needs of Black women, many of whom have never been touched by their white doctors. Brenda and Wanda have begun providing clothing, transportation, information, and referral services for these women.

The Hensons both feel the toll of their years of advocacy and activism. Wanda has been diagnosed with post-traumatic stress syndrome, and Brenda has been fighting colon cancer.

---

[38] Scanlan Stefanakos.

The Hensons are often asked why they chose to settle and establish their organization in the hostile climate of rural Mississippi. Wanda replies, "Why not in Mississippi, the poorest state in the nation and the most oppressed? It's where I was born, it's where I'm from". Brenda says, "They don't need Camp Sister Spirit in California".

> The major lesson we learned – and the reason we could not get into court to stop the aggression against us in the first few years – is that there are no civil rights laws to protect us as lesbians and gays....I feel that the United States is in violation of the international human rights laws which mandate governments to protect their citizens from being terrorized. As global citizens we have the right to live without fear. Yet fear is a way of life for many gays and lesbians here in the US; just see how many of them are closeted. I can't tell you how many times African American Mississippians have stopped us in town and said, with an air of hope and of trying to get us to understand the real issue, 'Listen, this is what it is. We got our rights. You can get yours too. Keep on going'.

Cheri Honkala
Philadelphia

"While freedom and democracy are celebrated today, the poor still live in terror, with no right to healthcare, food, affordable housing, or a job at a living wage. They are trying to drown out our voices, but we will be heard" – Cheri Honkala[39]

Cheri Honkala is the executive director of the Kensington Welfare Rights Union (KWRU), a mother, teacher, and social worker. She has been homeless three times and until four years ago was a welfare recipient.

Based in Philadelphia, the Kensington Welfare Rights Union is a non-violent, multi-racial organization of poor and homeless families. For twelve years it has been developing leaders from among the ranks of the poor and fighting to secure basic human needs for poor men, women, and children in the United States.

Honkala has been arrested over eighty times. She has faced four felony charges carrying a potential for twenty years in prison. Repercussions for Honkala's activities have also been visited upon her son. At the age of 13, he was arrested at a homeless demonstration. He was stripped and subjected to an intrusive body-cavity search. He subsequently filed a lawsuit against the city that led to a change in the law to prevent such searches.

On US Independence Day, July 4, 2003, the city of Philadelphia held a celebration for the opening of Constitution Center, a new facility housing the Liberty Bell, a venerated symbol of the American Revolution. Poor and homeless families from Philadelphia planned to take advantage of the event by holding a peaceful protest to demand their economic human rights.

As the demonstrators marched toward Constitution Center single-file, carrying their own mattresses and led by children, park rangers, federal guards, and city police formed lines to prevent the families from approaching. Singing "We Shall Not Be Moved", the demonstrators locked arms and refused to leave the sidewalk.

---

[39] Material for this section was gathered from interviews with members of the Kensington Welfare Rights Union in 2003.

Protest leaders Honkala and Galen Tyler had prepared a "Declaration of Economic Human Rights" to present at the Center. As they moved toward the Center, police moved to stop them, threw them to the ground, handcuffed them, and placed them under arrest. Honkala and Galen spent the night in jail, charged with multiple felony and misdemeanor offenses, including disorderly conduct, resisting arrest, and assaulting a police officer.

Honkala was charged with one first-degree felony and four other felony counts. Police officers claimed that Honkala had struck one of them in the chest. However, a video taken at the time clearly shows Honkala carrying a mattress and being struck by the officer. In subsequent hearings, it became clear that a whole room full of police officers conspired to concoct charges against Honkala and Tyler, but all the charges were subsequently withdrawn by the District Attorney's office.

* * *

Cheri Honkala grew up poor in Minneapolis, Minnesota. Her mother, a victim of domestic violence and abuse, was classified as an unfit parent. From the age of 13, Honkala was placed in nine different juvenile institutions. At 16, she says she became pregnant as a way of avoiding more institutions.

She persuaded a car dealer to sell her a car; she lived in it while pregnant. When she lost the car, she could not find shelter in the winter. Forced to move from one short-term place to another, she still managed to complete high school. She got a job and lost it. She began living in abandoned, unheated structures until her first son was born in 1981. After that it became too frightening to continue to find vacant housing on her own, so she teamed up with other women she met in a welfare office. Thus, she says, her work with homeless families began as a matter of personal necessity.

As she became more aware of the political dimensions of her personal situation, she began to see more and more people living in similar conditions. Seeing so many people getting "kicked around" so often, she began to ask herself, "How do they [official authorities] get away with it?" The more organizations she went to for assistance, the more she heard that homelessness "is not our issue". Honkala describes herself in those years as having a hard time understanding how so much money could be spent on the military and so little on the needs of the homeless.

In the late 1980s, Honkala became a key activist with Up and Out of Poverty Now, an organization based in Minneapolis that took over vacant buildings to be used as housing for homeless families. Eventually, Honkala was given space in the Minneapolis office of Women Against Military Madness, and began merging her personal and political concerns.

As a result of her political activity, she was ultimately prevented from obtaining housing in Minneapolis. When a relationship developed with a union official in Philadelphia, she decided to marry and move there with her young son. They settled in the Kensington neighborhood, the origin of the famous march in which the famous union organizer Mother Jones led a group of children who had lost fingers in industrial accidents to New York to protest the treatment of children used to fill industrial jobs.

Like many inner city neighborhoods in the USA, Kensington has always had a difficult time of it. Kensington's decline began with the loss of textile and brewing jobs to cheap labor pools overseas. Poverty and homelessness rose. Galen Tyler, chair of KWRU's Organizing Committee, says, "Welfare and drugs are the two biggest sources of incomes in Kensington".

In Philadelphia Honkala became a juvenile social worker. When she protested inadequacies in the treatment of a particular case, she was laid off. When she found herself again poor, without a job, and with the responsibility for a young son, she had to turn to welfare.

However, she refused to sign the Pennsylvania Agreement of Mutual Responsibility (AMR) because it essentially absolved the state of responsibility for childcare, health care, and employment assistance for parents who were receiving welfare. As a consequence, she was permanently sanctioned from receiving cash assistance from the welfare authorities.

In 1991 along with five other women, Cheri Honkala founded the Kensington Welfare Rights Union in the basement of a church. She says that she simply needed to join with other women to prevent her own homelessness, but this personal survival effort soon became a movement on behalf of all poor and homeless people.

Honkala sums up her work and her life this way:

The reality is I miss a normal life, whatever that is. I'm not a martyr. There's very little romanticism about this work. I would love to go on vacation, I would love to go shopping, buy my son things, and I'd love to have paid my rent for the last two months. However, I think that there are many fundamental things that happened to me in my life that knocked me so down, from growing up and being taken away from my mother to pulling myself up by my bootstraps in this country and then becoming homeless with my son, and then burying tons and tons of people as a direct result of being poor. Those are the things that really make me who I am, and give me strength to not take the easy way out. Actually, it really wouldn't work for me. I think that once you have your eyes opened, and you see what's happening in this world…for me I can't go back. I might be able to handle working in one of those kinds of jobs for maybe a few weeks or whatever, but I would go insane. There's something deeper that I would lose in that process. Right now, I may not have any money. However, I sleep well at night, and I can get up every morning and feel good about who I am. I really feel like I'm totally alive. I think that even though I don't have money, I have something that a whole lot of people strive their whole life for, which is to live life to the fullest.

* * *

In 1991 the Kensington Welfare Rights Union took over an abandoned welfare office where drugs were being sold. They cleaned it up to create a community center for the children of homeless parents. They were arrested and charged with fifteen counts carrying the potential for fifteen years in prison; they were acquitted.

KWRU developed a constant commitment to salvaging excess housing in Philadelphia in order to provide shelter for homeless families. Honkala points out that while there is little affordable housing in Philadelphia, there is more abandoned housing than there are homeless families. KWRU has emphasized the acquisition of vacant government-owned housing and the resettling of homeless pregnant women and families.

Such activity is illegal, even when buildings are apparently permanently abandoned. Honkala and her colleagues are arrested over and over, and then negotiate for their release and for use of the properties. In this way they have secured over five hundred properties for use by homeless residents.

Honkala says, "There's no reason for hunger and homelessness. They can put up stadiums and entertainment centers – they can build houses too".

The main actions of KWRU follow a pattern: they identify an abandoned property, usually owned by the Department of Housing and Urban Development (HUD). They move homeless families into the property. The police arrive, sometimes within hours, sometimes as long as two years later. Depending on whether the housing is owned by the municipal or Federal Government, any one of a number of law-enforcement agencies may be involved: local police, federal marshals, the Federal Bureau of Investigation (FBI), or the Office of Civil Affairs, an agency of the Philadelphia police that monitors and investigates local groups, similar to the FBI's national role. KWRU fills the house with students, religious leaders, and community activists willing to be arrested for the cause and committed to non-violent civil disobedience. Sometimes there is no action at all; sometimes everyone goes to jail for days. The variation seems to reflect the prevailing political expediency of the moment. Sometimes the families are resettled in other housing, either by city or federal housing authorities, or by private donors.

KWRU also sets up homeless encampments. They identify a plot of vacant land at a spot that will be sure to draw attention. They erect shantytowns of sixty or more homeless families and name them after prominent officials responsible for perpetuating poverty. They have also taken over abandoned churches and been arrested in the company of nuns.

Honkala describes KWRU's actions this way:

> Daily we're engaged in using what we call our "human rights house" right now to make plans on where the abandoned houses are in the Philadelphia area. We take poor and homeless families through the training on how to do a take-over. We

identify abandoned properties that are owned by Housing and Urban Development [the Federal housing agency], and we go out to the properties. We move the families in, and the families usually live there from anywhere from four to six months. There's usually a great deal of police activity during those four to six months, but we know that those properties are under the jurisdiction of the Federal Government, and that they have to send out Federal Marshals in order to evict families from those properties. We do it because we feel like we're morally justified, that if the City of Philadelphia can't house these families then we intend to house them ourselves....What would it be like to live in a cooperative society? And we try to demonstrate that, and live that every day of our lives, through free food distribution. Where food would normally be thrown away, we distributed it. Where empty houses would remain empty, we try and fill those houses. So, we try to live cooperatively and model our everyday lives after a much larger vision of a new kind of world that we'd like to live in.

In August of 1996, then President Clinton signed "welfare reform" into law, essentially removing the federal safety net for poor people that had been in place for over sixty years. Under the Temporary Assistance to Needy Families (TANF) reform plan, all "able-bodied" welfare recipients are required to work at least twenty hours a week in order to receive benefits, a system similar to what had been known as "workfare". In practice, for most people who receive assistance this means wages at or below minimum wage, with no benefits and without the basic safety, health, and civil rights protections other employees are guaranteed. Workers are rarely able to unionize and are sometimes used to replace union workers.

In response Cheri Honkala and other members of the Kensington Welfare Rights Union intensified their efforts to make poverty a human rights issue, not just in Philadelphia but across the country. Their strategies included highly visible marches, national tours, and tent encampments. In July 1997, KWRU organized the *March for Our Lives* from the Liberty Bell in Philadelphia to the United Nations in New York to protest human rights violations in the USA caused by welfare reform. This event served as the launch of the Poor People's Economic Human Rights Campaign, initiated by

KWRU and linking over one hundred organizations of poor people from across the USA. Honkala said,

> Those of us who have slept on the sidewalks can see the numbers [of homeless] growing. The fastest growing segment of the homeless in the US is families with children. Families who must go daily and wait in line from early morning until six at night, praying and hoping that the shelter provider calls out their name. Meaning they and their children have been chosen for the few remaining beds for that night.

In the summer of 1999, KWRU led a series of housing takeovers and set up tent cities to address a growing crisis of affordable housing and poverty in Philadelphia. After being charged with multiple felonies for attempting to rehabilitate abandoned houses and being ejected from Independence Mall near the Liberty Bell, they set up "Clintonville", a tent city where families lived until they could secure affordable housing.

Other marches followed. In October 1999, KWRU led organizations of the poor and homeless from across the USA, as well as Canada and Latin America, on a "March of the Americas" from Washington, DC, to the United Nations in New York to protest economic human rights violations. Another march in July of 2000 drew 10,000 homeless and poor people from around the country for the opening day of the Republican Party's National Convention in Philadelphia. Of several protest marches, this "March for Economic Human Rights" was the only one denied a permit by city authorities. From November 10 to December 10, 2002, the Poor People's Economic Rights Campaign organized a second national bus tour of the USA. Poor, unemployed, and working families traveled across the country to document and protest economic human rights violations.

Following the disrupted July 4, 2003, demonstration in Philadelphia, KWRU led the Poor People's Economic Human Rights Campaign on an epic march from Marks, Mississippi to Washington, DC. Timed to commemorate the thirty-fifth anniversary of the Poor People's Campaign that Dr. Martin Luther King was planning when he was assassinated, they arrived in Washington on the fortieth anniversary of King's "I Have a Dream" speech. The marchers called upon the memory of Dr. King, who once asked, "What does it profit a man to be able to eat at an integrated lunch counter if he doesn't have enough money to buy a hamburger?" The marchers erected an encampment on the National Mall they dubbed "Bushville". Honkala and other march leaders were arrested the day they arrived and held for two days. They were banned from setting foot on the Mall on threat of six months in jail.

And KWRU continues to march. They are preparing to lead a massive poor people's march on the first day of the Republican National Convention in New York City, in September of 2004.

In June of 1998 KWRU organized its first national bus tour. New Freedom Bus Tour traveled across the United States, gathering stories of economic human rights violations to present to the United Nations. Poor and homeless families visited thirty-five poor urban and rural communities. Says Honkala, "We turned ourselves into human rights monitors and began to document hidden stories of economic human rights violations". A second bus tour, the Poor People's Economic Human Rights Campaign, followed in late November, 2002, carrying unemployed and working families to twenty-seven cities to document and protest economic human rights violations.

Through all of these national events, KWRU has continued its day-to-day work in Philadelphia. They have established several "Human Rights Houses", which serve as bases for education and organizing. They house families, distribute food and clothing, and respond to the needs of poor people in the community. They have set up a "Human Rights Center" in Kensington that offers literacy and leadership classes, political education, and welfare advocacy. Honkala and the KWRU continue to move homeless families into abandoned houses. They teach similar tactics to homeless and poor activists throughout the USA.

As a result of these activities, law-enforcement authorities from around the country view Honkala as a threat to business as usual. When a major event occurs anywhere in the USA that has anything to do with economic rights, Honkala is likely to be subjected to pre-emptive arrest. At the time of the demonstrations against the World Trade Organization (WTO) meeting in Seattle in 2002, Honkala was the first person to be arrested. (Seattle is 3,000 miles from Philadelphia.) Again she was charged with assaulting an officer, charges that were dropped.

The behavior of the Philadelphia police at peaceful demonstrations and events like those of KWRU has long been the subject of criticism and investigation. Such behavior is marked by the following characteristics:

1) pre-emptive arrests of potential leaders or participants;
2) erecting blockades to prevent demonstrators from taking up positions for which they have received permits;
3) unnecessarily aggressive behavior, including taunting, insults, pushing, and beating;
4) those arrested are given unusually high bail fees;
5) rather than receiving the customary citation, demonstrators are held for relatively long periods (e.g. two days) in poor conditions;
6) at interrogation, police use questions about the highly controversial Philadelphia death-row inmate Mumia Abu-Jamal as a political litmus test.

In a move that Honkala views as attempted suborning of her work, the Mayor of Philadelphia offered Honkala a job that would have paid her in excess of $100,000 per year to oversee homeless programs. She turned it down.

When charged as a result of their activities, Honkala and her colleagues are frequently unable to secure legal representation. Depending on the political climate, law firms and individual defenders are intimidated from taking cases related to her work.

The charges currently pending against Honkala include a trespass charge for setting up a "Naftaville" shanty town at a factory in North Carolina that had lost 4500 jobs to other countries as a consequence of the North American Free Trade Agreement; she is also charged with trespass and disorderly conduct in consequence of two separate arrests on the National Mall in Washington DC.

KWRU has filed a lawsuit against the Philadelphia Police Department as a result of the arrests of Honkala and Tyler on July 4, 2000.

Honkala and her colleagues consciously use the Universal Declaration of Human Rights as an international tool, especially its protections and guarantees of international economic, social, and cultural rights. Honkala traces their recognition of their human rights to a cold night in October of

1995, when she and other homeless people were living on the steps of the state capitol building in Harrisburg, Pennsylvania. The Governor, Tom Ridge (now President Bush's Secretary of Homeland Security), ordered guards to remove the protesters' blankets. The people on the steps began talking about feeling less than human; this led to a discussion of how much they needed to be accorded basic rights as human beings. This in turn led activists to explore international human rights law, and to reach out to the international community. Honkala has said,

> We see this growing poverty as a direct violation of Articles 23, 25, and 26 of the Universal Declaration of Human Rights, and Section 1, Paragraph 30 of the Vienna Declaration and Program of Action regarding 'Poverty, hunger and other denials of economic, social and cultural rights'.

From April 12 to 16, 2004, Honkala was the only US delegate in an emergency delegation of human rights defenders from the Americas to Venezuela. The delegation's intent was to protect the human rights advances in Venezuela in health care, housing and education, threatened by foreign and domestic forces seeking to undermine the Government. Said Honkala, "I believe in democracy, nonviolence, freedom of the press, freedom of speech and basic human rights, and I am disturbed by the dismantling of those principles both in my own country and abroad".

* * *

The United Nations Declaration on Human Rights Defenders states in Article 1 that "everyone has the right, individually and in association with others, to promote and to strive for the protection and realization of human rights and fundamental freedoms at the national and international levels". Article 2 states that

> Each State has a prime responsibility and duty to protect, promote and implement **all** human rights and fundamental freedoms, *inter alia*, by adopting such steps as may be necessary to create all conditions necessary in the **social, economic**, political and other fields, as well as the legal guarantees required to ensure that all persons under its

jurisdiction, individually and in association with others, are able to enjoy all those rights and freedoms **in practice** (emphasis added).

Article 12 of the Declaration further states "everyone has the right, individually and in association with others, to participate in peaceful activities against violations of human rights and fundamental freedoms".

KWRU not only works in the name of international human rights standards, but also relies on international solidarity to survive. Honkala is convinced that were it not for KWRU's website[40] being accessed by activists in other parts of the world, the Government would have eliminated KWRU by now. Even so, Honkala believes that within two years she will be serving a long prison term as a consequence for her activism.

Honkala is convinced that the system of controls available to the US Government is far less visible and in some ways more intimidating than methods of repression used by governments more frequently sanctioned by the international community.

Honkala fears the consequences for the movement for economic justice in the USA will fail unless some combination of the following occurs:
1) the movement for economic justice in the USA receives the spotlight of concern from outside the US;
2) human rights monitors are dispatched to the USA to protect the poor, homeless and related activists;
3) an urgent alert system is devised to draw condemnation from other countries when a violation occurs in the USA;
4) there is a concerted challenge to the perception, widespread in the world, that the USA basks in civil liberties.

Honkala believes that there is an urgent need for international human rights monitors to be present at poverty-related demonstrations, marches, and events in the USA. She says there is also a need for international observation of hearings and trials, especially when defendants have been unable to secure adequate legal representation.

---

[40] http://www.kwru.org

Chokwe Lumumba
Detroit, Michigan and Jackson, Mississippi

"I only came to the movement because of King and he was killed. I only stayed in the movement because of Malcolm and he was killed. Then I became a leader" – Chokwe Lumumba

At the age of 60, Chokwe Lumumba is well into his fifth decade as an activist, attorney, and human rights advocate. He began civil rights activism in high school in the 1950s, and since 1968 he has included the language and principles of international human rights in his work.

Throughout his life Lumumba has worked to defend the rights of African American activists and communities. He has educated and organized student activists throughout the Midwest and the South and persuaded universities to attract and cultivate people of color. He has been on the frontline of protecting African American communities from drug trafficking and gang violence. He has opposed rights violations by local, state, and national law enforcement and intelligence agencies and vigilante groups; he has confronted the Ku Klux Klan in Michigan and Mississippi.

As an attorney Lumumba has played a leading role in many significant cases over the last twenty-five years, representing poor people and political activists and defending individuals and groups whose human rights have been violated. He has fought against the death penalty in general and against executions in individual cases.

Over the years Lumumba and members of his family have been harassed, threatened, and arrested for the role he has played in these struggles. The Federal Bureau of Investigation (FBI) and other law enforcement agencies have surveyed his activities. He has suffered discrimination when trying to rent and buy property. He has been prevented from practicing law and now is facing the loss of his license to practice in Mississippi in circumstances that suggest that his political activities and speech are the reason.

* * *

Chokwe Lumumba was born in 1943 into a family of seven brothers and sisters in the public housing projects of Detroit's West Side. Originally named Edwin Taliaferro, he later renounced this as a "slave name" in favor of *Lumumba,* after the Congolese nationalist and prime minister, and *Chokwe,* the name of an Angolan tribe. His early education was in Catholic schools, where blatant racism was part of the learning experience:

> I remember going to a white church….and a guy asked me and my brother, 'Why are you niggers going to this church?' Later on a white guy told me with conviction that God had left me in the oven too long. It occurred to me that whites were spending their time teaching their children racism.

At Saint Theresa High School, where he was student council president and captain of the football team, he began to engage in political protest activities. He and his mother would stand on street corners to collect money to support the activities of the Student National Coordinating Committee (SNCC), a primarily African American organization promoting respect for civil rights throughout the South. A speech given by Martin Luther King in 1963 inspired Lumumba to make civil rights his life's work.

Dr. King's assassination on April 4, 1968, affected Lumumba profoundly. He says, "I think the single most important thing in my political development is his death. You see, to my mother he was the Black Moses. She followed him and she always talked to me about him". On the day following King's death, Lumumba, participated in a student takeover of the University Center Building of Western Michigan University, where he was a student. The protesters demanded that the university hire more African American teachers and create Martin Luther King scholarships for African American students.

Lumumba became part of the movement to establish African American studies programs at other universities throughout the Midwest and he helped organize Black student movements in Michigan, Ohio, and Indiana. He formed the Black United Front at Kalamazoo College in western Michigan, forcing a shift of resources from buildings to childhood education in the predominantly African American area of Kalamazoo, Michigan.

In 1969 Lumumba entered law school at Wayne State University in Detroit. In the first year, however, eighteen of the twenty-four Black students in his class failed due to a discriminatory grading system. In response to this injustice, Lumumba and other Black students occupied the law school administration building demanding reinstatement of the students and fair grading practices. As a result Wayne State readmitted the students and established an anonymous system of grading. Ultimately all but two of the students received good grades and graduated, many of them becoming prominent attorneys and judges. Lumumba himself graduated *cum laude* in 1975. Lumumba continued his advocacy of equal education at Wayne State and has supported programs that allow African American students to succeed in the law school environment.

After graduation, Lumumba became an advocate for the protection of Black communities, following attacks by local police and vigilante groups. Rather than harassing the so-called "radical leadership", special units of the Detroit police, had begun targeting the African American community for "pre-emptive action".

Lumumba confronted these abuses with community patrols against violence and drug dealing and an urban scout program for young people to protect themselves against gang and racial attacks. He created the Malcolm X Center to educate and train young Black activists. He established Africa-centric schools to teach the dismantling of racism and sexism and inspire Black pride. He challenged the excessive rates for heat and electricity being charged residents of poor neighborhoods.

In the early 1970s in a case of national prominence, Lumumba defended Hayward Brown, a radical Black activist who had previously been acquitted of assaulting a police officer. Lumumba defended Brown on charges of possession of a concealed weapon in the virtually all-white suburb of Dearborn, Michigan. When a jury of nine Blacks and three whites could not reach a verdict, Lumumba declared,

> The Wayne County prosecutor has chased Haywood Brown relentlessly from jury to jury, from judge to judge and from court to court with trumped-up charges....Not only are his human rights being violated, ours are likewise. They are using

our tax dollars in their endeavor to silence another freedom fighter.[41]

Also at this time Lumumba became vice-president of the Republic of New Afrika (RNA), an organization formed to coordinate the efforts of individual activists, Black nationalists, and grassroots groups of diverse philosophies. The RNA was staunchly anti-capitalist, sought reparations for slavery, and aimed at giving African Americans control over their lives and land. Although the RNA drew support from prominent civil rights figures like Congressman Julian Bond and comedian Dick Gregory, it became a key target of the FBI's Cointelpro program, a system of illegal government subversion intended to destroy groups perceived to be a threat to the USA. They followed him throughout the country, attempted to recruit a cousin to spy on him, and kept constant watch on his mother's house.[42]

Not surprisingly this kind of advocacy and activism had consequences for Lumumba and his family. In September of 1971, he was arrested during a citywide sweep after the murder of a Detroit police officer. While he was being booked, police officers referred to his involvement with the RNA saying, "We're going to send you all back to Africa in boxes with African names on them". Lumumba's younger brother, then 13, was arrested and held in jail but never charged. Police have made a point of informing Lumumba's landlords of his past political activities.

In 1972 the RNA purchased land near Jackson, Mississippi, as the geographic base for the movement. The RNA met with discrimination, threats, harassment, roadblocks, and arrests by local, state, and federal law enforcement agencies. Lumumba took responsibility for confronting and negotiating with theses agencies and managed to convince the FBI to order the removal of roadblocks preventing access to the land. Local police and the FBI mounted an assault on a house that was serving as RNA headquarters in Jackson. In 1973, Mississippi police officers stopped Lumumba and his wife while they were out for a walk; he recalls, "They put a shotgun in my gut and asked, 'Are you the second-in-charge of the black-ass niggers?'"

---

[41] *New Afrikan*, February 1979.

[42] From documents released at Lumumba's request under the Freedom of Information Act.

Back in Detroit in 1976, Lumumba joined the staff of the Detroit Public Defenders Office, providing free counsel to indigent clients. In 1978 he set up his own law firm with the intention of combining his political advocacy with his legal skills. He sued Wayne State University for abandoning their program of affirmative action in admitting African American students. He defended Alton Maddox, a prominent police-abuse attorney suspended by the Michigan Bar Association because he refused to give authorities information about a client.

On July 22, 1978, inmates at the maximum security prison in Pontiac, Illinois rioted to protest violations against prisoner rights, including unsanitary living conditions; cramped quarters; cold, insect-infested food; lack of medical treatment; and guard brutality. Many prisoners were injured and three guards were killed in the riot; twenty-eight African Americans and three Latinos were charged. Sixteen of the accused, popularly known as the "Pontiac Sixteen", faced murder charges and a possible death sentence if convicted. Lumumba agreed to defend Ozzie Williams, whom he perceived to be one of the most political of those charged, in this significant case. Eventually, all charges against the defendants were dismissed. Lumumba said at the time, "The Pontiac Sixteen trial is … the type of case that I got into the legal profession to deal with". At trial ten of the Pontiac Sixteen were found not guilty; all charges against the other defendants were dismissed.

Lumumba was an organizer of and speaker at the February 1980 New York City march for the rights of African Americans. Five thousand people walked from Harlem to the United Nations Building to demand an international forum on the plight of minority populations in the US.

He was lead defense counsel in the "Brinks Case", a major legal confrontation between the Justice Department and a group of revolutionaries who had been charged with the October 1981 robbery of $1.6 million from an armored car and the killing of two police officers and a guard in Rockland County, New York. On November 10, 1981, New York Judge Irving Ben Cooper barred Lumumba from representing Fulani Sunni Ali (Cynthia Boston) on charges arising from the Brink's incident, citing his political ideology, his values as a lawyer, and his behavior on the witness stand. Of this ruling Stephen Shapiro, then chief counsel for the New York Civil Liberties Union said, "The opinion incredibly ignores two sacred rights in this country: the right to free speech and association, and the right of a criminal defendant to choose her own lawyer". Lumumba ultimately won the right to represent Fulani Sunni Ali and her husband, Bilal Sunni Ali. The charges against Fulani were ultimately dismissed when witnesses established her whereabouts in New Orleans at the time of the Brink's incident in New York.[43]

On September 3, 1983, the Brinks Case ended in a stunning defeat for the US Government. Six of the eight defendants were acquitted of all major charges, and no defendant was convicted in the actual robbery. As a result of his comments to the press, Lumumba was held in contempt by the District Judge.

In 1985 Lumumba worked with a legal team that successfully uncovered evidence demonstrating how the FBI targeted and framed activist Geronimo Pratt. That work ultimately helped win Pratt's release ten years later. In similar cases he defended Asata Shakur, Mutulu Shakur, and Mutulu's son, the popular music performer Tupac Shakur. In 1991 he represented activists in Los Angeles protesting the videotaped police beating of a young Black man named Rodney King. Lumumba notes with pride that most of his political clients have gone on to become effective activists; Geronimo Pratt, for example, now works as a community development advocate in Louisiana and Africa.

In 1985 Lumumba became active in the movement against apartheid in South Africa, training and motivating young people to become active in "fighting for something other than drug turf".

* * *

When Lumumba returned to Mississippi in 1988, his application to practice law in the state was held in limbo for three years. But he rapidly became a noted legal and community advocate, focusing on clients who had experienced violations of their fundamental human rights. For example, he defended DeWayne Boyd, a civil rights activist who had helped to sue the US Department of Agriculture for reparations for African Americans.

---

[43] Stephen Braun, 'His Practice Is to Mix Law and Revolution', *Detroit Free Press*, 20 October 1982.

Lumumba offered his protection to Boyd, who was in Mississippi trying to prevent the illegal expropriation of African American-owned land.

After he was granted the right to practice law in 1991, Lumumba represented the family of Johnnie Griffin, a community activist who had been shot by the police, in a wrongful-death suit. A self-avowed segregationist police officer shot Griffin to death at his home in front of his four children. Lumumba won $250,000 in compensatory damages for the family.

In the 1990s Lumumba increasingly specialized in cases where racial prejudice and political power combine to produce biased investigations, unjust arrests, and excessively punitive sentences. In a landmark case for Mississippi, he wins the acquittal of George Little, a young African American charged with murder for defending himself against an attack by a white man.

In July of 1995, 13-year-old Elliot Culp was one of several witnesses to the murder of a white woman by a white man. Although Culp had reported what he saw to police, they chose not to investigate the perpetrator but to arrest Culp instead. The teenager spent one year in prison charged with capital murder before Lumumba won his acquittal and release. Lumumba said at the time of Culp's release, "This verdict is a triumph over thoughtless, narrow-minded advocates for wholesale execution and wholesale incarceration of our children".[44]

In February of 1996, Lumumba announced that he would pursue lawsuits on behalf of Charles and Esther Quinn. A few days after the Quinns' son Andre Jones had been arrested in August of 1992, he was found hanged in a shower stall in the Simpson County jail. The case attracted national attention for three reasons: first because he was one of the last of forty-eight jailhouse hangings of young African American men in Mississippi since 1987; second, because an independent autopsy ruled the death a homicide after state's pathologist had called it a suicide; and finally, because the hanging happened under the supervision of Simpson County Sheriff Lloyd "Goon" Jones. Jones had become infamous after being accused in the deaths of two foreign journalists covering the landmark racial integration admission of James Meredith to the University of Mississippi in 1962. Jones was later

---

[44] Charles Tisdale, 'Culp Acquitted of Murder', *Jackson Advocate*, August 1996.

implicated in the murders of two Jackson State University students in 1972. Lumumba won substantial damages for the Quinn family.

In the mid-1990s Lumumba took on the system of capital punishment in Mississippi. Typically defendants in capital cases, predominantly African-Americans, have little access to information or competent counsel. In their fear and vulnerability, they frequently follow the advice of prosecutors to plead guilty and serve life in prison, rather than "take their chances with a jury and get death". Death sentences and executions in the USA are plagued by: racial disparities, execution of juvenile and mentally disabled prisoners, and conviction of people who are later found to be innocent.

When Lumumba observes that in over ninety percent of his cases the defendant is either found not guilty or his death sentence is reversed, he stresses that any good, independent attorney would have the same results. However, most poor defendants receive totally ineffective counsel because of the system of representation in effect in Mississippi is not designed to ensure effective representation of defendants in these complex cases.

According to Lumumba, the case of John Buford Irving is typical. Irving was convicted and sentenced to death for shooting a white storeowner during an alleged 1976 robbery when he was 17-years-old. After Lumumba took up the case, secured a new sentencing hearing, and won a change of venue. Irving's death sentence was reversed. Lumumba notes that in prison Irving has developed into an advocate for other prisoners, often writing their appellate briefs.

Lumumba has consistently participated in demonstrations against the activities of the Ku Klux Klan. In 1990 he represented anti-Klan demonstrators accused of infringing on the Klan's civil rights. As a demonstrator and outspoken advocate, Lumumba has had police protecting the Klan point their guns directly at him. He has also defended groups of anti-Klan demonstrators in other parts of the country.

The Mississippi legal establishment has also directed its hostility against him. In 2000 the Mississippi Bar publicly reprimanded Lumumba for speaking out against Hinds County Circuit Judge Swan Yerger. A self-proclaimed segregationist, Yerger had dismissed a lawsuit filed against a white police officer brought by Lumumba for an African American client.

Lumumba challenged the judge's decision as being discriminatory. Judge Yerger held him in contempt and filed a complaint with the Mississippi Bar.

* * *

Lumumba is currently embroiled in a fight for professional survival, facing the potential loss of his ability to practice law in Mississippi. In the summer of 1996, an African American named Henry Payton came before Judge Marcus Gordon of the Leake County Circuit Court in Carthage, Mississippi. Payton was convicted of bank robbery and arson and sentenced to five years in prison. However, the conviction was overturned by the Mississippi Supreme Court, which found that Judge Gordon had violated Payton's rights in the trial. The case was returned to Gordon for a new trial; Payton hired Lumumba to defend him.[45]

According to reports, during the trial Judge Gordon openly expressed animosity toward Lumumba and bias against Payton. Lumumba requested that the judge disqualify himself; the judge refused. When the jury was unable to reach a verdict, Gordon ordered them to deliberate further and two hours later the jury returned with a verdict of guilty. This time, Judge Gordon gave Payton a sentence of forty-eight years in prison.

After the trial several jurors said that they would not have found Payton guilty, but had understood the judge's instructions to mean that the law required them to put aside their honest beliefs to reach a verdict. Other jurors admitted that they were acquainted with one of the prosecution's key witnesses and had decided that Payton was guilty before the trial began.

In October 2001, Lumumba filed a motion for a new trial. At the hearing Judge Gordon would not allow any of the jurors to testify and refused to order the appearance of people with knowledge of jury misconduct. Lumumba accused Gordon of being unfair. Later Lumumba told a reporter that Gordon "had the judicial demeanor of a barbarian". He was held in contempt, ejected from the courtroom and jailed for three days. He was fined $300 for saying he was proud to be removed from the courtroom, and $500 for "failing to demonstrate contrition".

---

[45] 'Marcus Gordon and the Mississippi Bar vs. Chokwe Lumumba', *Bamn News*, September 2002.

On April 10, 2003, two lawyers and a judge from Harrison County, Mississippi, formed a tribunal and held a hearing on the charges. Lumumba explained that his comments during the Payton trial were prompted by the biased manner of Judge Gordon, including: allowing Payton to be brought before the jury in chains; cutting off Lumumba's *voir dire* of potential jurors; interrupting Lumumba's opening statement; reading erroneous instructions to the jury; and sentencing Payton to forty-eight years. One of Lumumba's attorneys argued that he had spoken out only with the intention of defending his client's rights, that the statement made about the judge's demeanor was protected as free speech, and that the transcript of the proceedings failed to show any evidence Lumumba had disrespected or disrupted the court. The tribunal found Lumumba guilty and ordered that he be publicly reprimanded.

The Mississippi Bar is apparently not satisfied with this reprimand and is appealing the tribunal's decision to the Mississippi Supreme Court, requesting a one year suspension — a punishment that would require Lumumba to give up all his clients and retake the state bar examination. A hearing was held on April 22, 2003, but a ruling has not yet been announced.[46]

In a separate proceeding, the Mississippi Supreme Court affirmed Lumumba's conviction for contempt of court. Leake County refused bond and he served three days in jail.

Lumumba says, "Of course the origin of these proceedings is political. It comes down to the Bar not wanting an assertive human rights lawyer who will challenge the various local courts and tribunals in Mississippi".

Though Front Line is not in a position to express an opinion on the merits of the pending proceedings, the circumstances of these charges against Lumumba raise substantial questions about whether he is being singled out for harsh treatment on the basis of his political beliefs and advocacy for unpopular clients and causes rather than his actual conduct in the courtroom.

* * *

---

[46] Nikki Burns, 'No Ruling Has Been Made on Lumumba's Disbarment Hearing', *Mississippi Link*, 24 April 2003. See also, Frank Imani Jamal, 'Chokwe Lumumba', *Michigan Citizen*, 25 January 2003

The United Nations Declaration on Human Rights Defenders states in Article 9 that everyone has the right

> To offer and provide professionally qualified legal assistance or other relevant advice and assistance in defending human rights and fundamental freedoms.... in the exercise of human rights and fundamental freedoms... everyone has the right... to benefit from an effective remedy and to be protected in the event of the violation of those rights.

* * *

Lumumba can recall his first moment of outrage at racism. In 1955 his mother showed him a magazine photograph: "It was a picture of the body of Emmett Till in *JET Magazine*". (The 14-year-old Till, an African American, had been kidnapped, tortured and murdered in rural Mississippi for whistling at a white woman).

> I said that they need to get the bad people that did that, and Mama said it wasn't just a few bad people, but America that was at fault. And this will eventually destroy it. I did not understood that at the time, but she said it in such a way that it stuck with me.

When asked if he considers himself a civil rights lawyer, Lumumba responds, "I am more fond of human rights, because human rights are what you have, regardless of who gives them to you".

Enrique Morones
San Diego, California

"They're chasing these people to death. If this was the Canadian border you wouldn't see this — no way" — Enrique Morones

At midnight on March 20, 1998, US-Mexican dual citizenship became available for the first time; at 12:01 *a.m.* on March 21, Enrique Morones petitioned for the status. In June of that year Morones became the first dual citizen of Mexico and the United States. His documents were presented to him personally by President Zedillo in a ceremony at the Mexican National Palace.

The status and the honor are entirely appropriate: throughout his forty-seven-year life, Enrique Morones has divided his heart and his soul between San Diego and Mexico. For over twenty years Enrique Morones has been an effective and vocal human rights defender for people in need on both sides of the border, and for nearly that long he has been a regional and national advocate for border activists and organizations.

For this work he has received many honors. But he has also received many threats on his life. He has been vilified by opposing politicians and news outlets. He has been shunned by potential business clients. And he was dismissed from the job he was born to do.

He is now a full-time advocate for Mexican immigrants to the USA, for the Hispanic community in and around San Diego, and for the human rights of all Latinos.[47]

* * *

Enrique Morones' father grew up in Mexico City, moving his family to San Diego in 1954. He worked for Aeromexico during the day and at a market at night to earn enough money to pay for a quality education for his five children. His wife of fifty-four years, who came from the Mexican town of Culiacan, instilled an appreciation for Mexican traditions and culture in the

---

[47] Unless otherwise cited, information on Enrique Morones is derived from interviews conducted with Morones in late 2003 and early 2004.

94

family, who still speak only Spanish at home. Enrique was the first member of the family to be born in the USA

Morones grew up in the working class San Diego neighborhood of Golden Hill. He attended St. Augustus High School, where he won the silver medal for academic achievement and became one of the finest long-distance runners in the USA. In 1979 he graduated from San Diego State University and in 2002 earned a master's degree in executive leadership from the University of San Diego.

A devout Roman Catholic, Morones draws his philosophy of servant leadership in protest and action to alleviate individual suffering from the example of Jesus Christ. Another early and continuing source of inspiration is his grandfather, Luis N. Morones, one of the founders of the labor movement in Mexico. His other exemplar is the late farm labor leader Cesar Chavez; Morones chairs the annual San Diego area tribute to Chavez.

Throughout his life Morones has divided his time and attention between Mexico and San Diego, which lies less than fifty kilometers from the Mexican border. Now the seventh largest city in the United States, San Diego has a population of 1,264,600[48], of which twenty-four percent is Hispanic. The city encompasses nearly 800 square kilometers and has more than one hundred kilometers of Pacific coastline.

The fastest growing minority in the USA, Hispanics are close to becoming the majority population in California. Some small towns in central California's agricultural heartland are now over ninety percent Latino. The Hispanic population of the USA may already equal the number of African Americans. The projected numbers for the year 2010 predict 190 million Latinos in a total US population of 570 million people.[49]

* * *

Many recent undocumented immigrants to the San Diego area work as manual laborers and service employees. To save money on housing, many

---

[48] US Census, 1 January 2002.
[49] *San Diego City Beat*, April 2003.

camp out in nearby canyons. In 1987 Enrique Morones founded Border Angels to provide these individuals and families with food and water.

Over the years, Border Angels has expanded its mission to include setting up and maintaining a series of stations in the desert border areas that separate Mexico from the Southwest United States. Each station is composed of a cross or light or other marker, six gallons of water, food and clothing. Border Angels now has over 600 active volunteers; with ten other groups they maintain over 1000 stations. Morones himself still makes regular deliveries to desert stations. The US Border Patrol is neutral on the aid stations. Morones has secured promises from border agents that they will not remove the contents of the stations or stake them out to apprehend migrants.

For decades, Mexican immigrants and migrants entering the United States without permission or documentation have chosen to cross the border on the coast near San Diego. Entering illegally has always involved risk: immigrants are misled or abandoned by smugglers called *coyotes*; they may be apprehended and treated badly by US Border Patrol agents; they may drown or be struck while crossing a freeway. But until 1993 crossing the border near San Diego brought immigrants a relatively short distance over mild terrain in comfortable weather to a major US city.

In 1994, however, the USA launched Operation Gatekeeper, a program of blocking and redirecting immigrant flows from Mexico. The program began with the building of a wall on the border between southern California and Mexico as well as increased surveillance by US Border Patrol agents. The wall consists of three parallel fences and a high-speed road. The fences are five meters high and cannot be climbed. They are set forty meters apart with the land between them denuded. The wall runs twenty kilometers from the Pacific to Otay Mesa, a town southwest of San Diego. Completion of the project will cost about $60 million.[50]

For eight years, Enrique Morones has been a leader of the opposition to Project Gatekeeper. He points out that the existence of the wall demands that individuals and families intent on crossing the border do so under far more difficult circumstances. The wall forces migrants to traverse 6000 foot

---

[50] Perlita Dicochea, 'Local Leaders Meet to Stop the Final Three Miles of the Triple Border Fence', *La Prensa San Diego*, 5 February 2004.

mountains where temperatures below freezing are likely for half of the year, or deserts with forty-five degree centigrade heat and ten meter sand dunes. And hundreds of immigrants have drowned trying to swim across the All-American Canal, a wide aqueduct.

Since the wall went up, 2650 people have died trying to enter California or Arizona, about one person per day. Half these deaths have been from exposure in the desert, most of those from heat stress, a long and excruciating event. As always, women and children are the most vulnerable.

Morones believes that Operation Gatekeeper was never intended to restrict illegal immigration, but to make it less visible and thereby less of a political liability. The strategy is to "redirect" migration traffic away from border cities and into the most remote, difficult, and dangerous terrain between San Diego and Brownsville, Texas, more than a thousand kilometers to the east.

Predictably, making illegal crossings more difficult and dangerous has done nothing to affect the flow of immigrants. In 1999, the American Civil Liberties Union and the California Rural Assistance Foundation filed a petition with the Organization of American States, charging that the US Government had failed to live up to its obligations by taking measures to maximize the physical risks accompanying immigration. UN High Commissioner for Human Rights, Mary Robinson, briefed on border deaths during a visit to Mexico, called the situation "shocking".

Since Operation Gatekeeper began, fewer than a dozen employers of undocumented workers have been prosecuted. In fact, only two percent of the enforcement work-hours of the Immigration and Naturalization Services are devoted to identifying employers suspected of hiring undocumented workers.[51]

Christian Ramirez, coordinator of border programs for the American Friends Service Committee says, "The fence creates a space of impunity for the Border Patrol. Within the fences there are no witnesses to human rights violations".

---

[51] US Government General Accounting Office, April 2002.

Morones says, "This fence gives the wrong message and it is hypocritical. The USA tells Gorbachev to take down their wall, and here our President has his". Morones considers it part of his advocacy work to bring the notions of international civil rights norms and protections to the border area in general and to the behavior of the Border Patrol in particular. There are approximately 10,000 Border Patrol agents in the USA; 3500 of those are assigned to the San Diego area. The Patrol has the lowest standards for entry-level employment (which includes carrying firearms) of any official US law enforcement agency.

Morones advocates and provides models for the training of Border Patrol agents in cultural diversity and human rights. He urges law enforcement officials to remember that the rights of people on the border should not be based on whether or not they are US citizens, but on the fundamental and universal rights of all men, women, and children.

Morones has also worked at the border between Arizona and Mexico. In Douglas, Arizona, he confronted vigilante groups organized to "hunt" immigrants. Says Morones, "You could feel the racism in the air". He met with the Governor and the state attorney general, promising a boycott of Arizona if the state did not provide better protections on the border.

Morones has hosted several fact-finding missions to the border by international human rights groups, including Human Rights Watch. On March 13, 2001, Gabriela Rodriquez Pizarro, the UN Special Rapporteur for Migrants, visited the border at San Diego. She was greeted by banners and crosses bearing the names of nearly 2000 immigrants known to have died between there and Brownsville, Texas.

* * *

Morones' advocacy has not been limited to border issues. The city of San Diego intends to erect a bronze statue of former mayor and California Governor Pete Wilson. Wilson was re-elected as Governor in large part because of his unqualified support for a ballot initiative called Proposition 187, which called for cutting services to undocumented immigrants, including health care and education. The initiative passed a popular referendum but was subsequently struck down by US courts as unconstitutional.

The proposition and the politicians like Pete Wilson who promoted it became anathema to the great majority of California's Hispanic population. Morones has blocked the installation of the statue and leads the opposition to prevent it from ever being erected. Morones has said,

> We cannot forget what he did with Proposition 187, how he divided the mainstream community from the Latino community and how he portrayed us like we were from another planet....When I see Pete Wilson, the first thing I think of is racism.

In 2000 Morones was selected by the Government of Mexico to monitor the Governor's election in the state of Chiapas and the elections in Mexico City that led to the presidency of Vicente Fox. He now participates in Fox's Institute of Mexicans Abroad, advising on legal issues relating to immigration. In this connection Morones is attempting to persuade the Mexican consulate in San Diego to take a more active role in protecting immigrants.

In 2001 Morones proposed a Casa Mexico pavilion to join similar country-themed educational centers in San Diego's Balboa Park. He pointed out that most of the centers in the park represented European countries. After two years of proposals, rejections, and compromises, Casa Mexico was established in November of 2003.

Five days a week Morones hosts a radio program in Spanish that provides the Hispanic community in and around San Diego with information and advice on immigration, health care, education, and legal issues. Morones dedicates each of his radio programs to someone who has died while crossing the border. He appears often on US television and radio advocating for the human rights of Mexican immigrants and by extension all immigrants and economic migrants.

* * *

Morones has had his share of recognition. In 1996 and 1997 he served as president of the San Diego County Hispanic Chamber of Commerce, which supports Latino businesses. In his two-year tenure he increased the number of member businesses from 100 to 850. He has been named one of the 100 most influential Latinos in the USA by both *Latino Impact* and *Hispania Business Magazine*. February 25, 1998 was declared Enrique Morones Day in both the city and the county of San Diego. He has won the Chicano Federation Community Service Award, Mexican Tourism's "Amigo de Baja" Award, and the Mexican Government's Foreign Affairs Award.

More often, however, Morones's advocacy has made him the object of abuse and retaliation rather than honors and recognition. For his work on border and immigration issues, Morones has received many death threats. For example, once while he was appearing on a television interview, a caller left a message on his home telephone: "I'm watching your TV show and I want to tell you that I think all Mexicans should die, especially you". Morones' answering machine captured the message and the caller's telephone number. However, when Morones contacted the Federal Bureau of Investigation (FBI), they claimed they could not offer assistance because the caller had not mentioned Morones' name. They did offer the gratuitous and disquieting observation that, "The ones you have to worry about are the ones who don't call".

He has been in other uncomfortable positions such as the visit to the taping of his radio show by a man wearing reflector sunglasses and a provocatively patriotic hat who simply glared at him and took notes. After addressing a meeting of the San Diego City Council on Latino opposition to the Wilson statue, Morones received a call saying that he was being followed and should stop his criticism of Wilson.

Morones has been severely criticized by politicians and journalists for what some see as providing encouragement to illegal immigration. His Casa Mexico project was nearly derailed when the approval committee confronted him with a dossier of his past political activities. Because of his advocacy and prominence, Morones has lost many potential business clients. Even business people who support the issues he advocates have second thoughts because they know that his first commitment is to those issues.

But no threats or ostracism or danger cuts as deeply as Morones' experience with the San Diego Padres baseball team.

In the United States, two institutions, largely out of self-interest, have played leading roles in breaking color lines and eliminating racial segregation: the military and sports. In 1994, the major league San Diego Padres baseball team was struggling to survive when it came under new ownership. After a series of letters and meetings Morones persuaded the owners that they could contribute to racial progress, build a new fan base, and become financially sound by doing one thing: embracing the Latino devotion to baseball.

In September of 1995, Morones joined the Padres organization and established the Department of Hispanic Marketing, the first such office in major-league baseball. He had enormous success in bringing professional US baseball teams to Mexico, and Mexican fans to San Diego. Over the course of six years, Morones increased the Padres' annual game-attending Latino following from 50,000 to 600,000 fans. In November of 2000, Morones was named Vice-President of Hispanic and International Marketing, becoming the first and only Latino vice-president in the Padres organization.

Then suddenly on October 30, 2001, Morones was fired and his position eliminated.

The firing was a devastating blow to Morones. A life-long fan of the Padres, he felt that being part of their organization while working to meet the needs of the Hispanic community in his hometown was the job of a lifetime. In the end he received no appreciation or recognition for his accomplishments. His reputation as a "troublemaker" prevented him from securing similar employment while his commitment to border issues made him unwilling to leave San Diego. With the Padres he had earned in excess of $100,000 per year; now he is heavily in debt.

After Morones was fired, the outcry in the Hispanic community was immediate, loud, and long. Newspaper columns, editorials, radio and television coverage blasted the Padres, but to no avail. The organization reneged on its promises to provide scholarships and build ball fields in Mexico. The team continues to lose its Latino fan base and its connection to the Hispanic population.

Writing in *Hispanic Vista*, the Latino commentator Luis Valdivia said,

The list of 'firsts' for Enrique Morones and his department is impressive. Never before had a major league team in any sport established a Hispanic marketing department, or opened a retail store outside the United States, or sold tickets at a discount outside the US, or facilitated transportation of fans across a border, or held a series of official games in Mexico, etcetera. And I do mean etcetera. The man should write a book.[52]

Morones has compensated by plunging even more deeply into his advocacy and activism. He emerged as a leader of the opposition in San Diego to the recall of California Governor Gray Davis and the subsequent election of conservative actor Arnold Schwarzenegger. He increased his level of involvement in preventing deaths on the border. Border Angels began building houses in Tijuana, donating goods to Casa del Migrante, and holding protests at prisons where immigrants are held.

In January of 2002, Morones and his volunteers began establishing cold-weather stations in the Cleveland National Forest, a mountainous area sixty kilometers to the east of San Diego. Each site is marked by a bright blue flag and a battery-powered red light. Each station contains blankets, sleeping bags, food and water. Morones has plans to set up similar stations in Yuma County, California and in the area around Tucson, Arizona.

In March of 2002, Morones established and became chair of the Border Commission, created to pressure the Mexican and US Governments to implement a more humane regimen on the border. Among its recommendations is the cessation of high-speed chases by Border Patrol agents and investigations into the cause of every death on the border.

* * *

The United Nations Declaration on Human Rights Defenders states in article 12 that "everyone has the right, individually and in association with others, to participate in peaceful activities against violations of human rights and fundamental freedoms".

---

[52] Luis Valdivia, *Hispanic Vista*, 7 January 2001.

Article 12 further states,

> The State shall take all necessary measures to ensure the protection by the competent authorities of everyone, individually and in association with others, against any violence, threats, retaliation, *de facto* or *de jure* adverse discrimination, pressure or any other arbitrary action as a consequence of his or her legitimate exercise of the rights referred to in the present Declaration.

Morones is currently president of Puentes Latinos, which represents Mexican businesses and organizations seeking access to US markets and sources of funding. His clients include the professional baseball team in Tijuana, the Hispanic Ad Council, and a Latina health care clinic at the University of California San Diego.

However, at the age of forty-seven, Morones finds himself alone, living in a two-room apartment. His advocacy and effectiveness continue unabated and he is sure that he "has done the right thing", but the personal costs and sacrifice have taken their toll on him.

Morones understands that the wall and the Border Patrol are only symptoms of the fundamental difficulty: the US and Mexico have not found an effective and humane strategy for addressing undocumented immigration. Although Mexico's economy is growing stronger, it cannot hope to compete with the allure of the USA.

Businesses in the USA need, encourage, and exploit less expensive immigrant workers. US consumers are unwilling to give up cheap prices, even on luxury goods, that would allow fair compensation to immigrants. And the farther one gets from the border area, the less concern there is about Mexican immigration. The issue rarely surfaces in national elections.

Referring to the history of the Southwest as Mexican until it was seized by the United States in 1848, Morones, says, "We didn't cross the border, the border crossed us".

Ken Riley & The Charleston Five
Charleston, South Carolina

"We are proof that working under a union contract can provide a living wage and that being organized means having political influence. That fact is what has scared those who want to maintain the old ways"

– Ken Riley, President ILA Local 1422

The Charleston Five are labor rights activists who were arrested and faced politically motivated charges of rioting, conspiracy to riot, and assaulting a police officer after a peaceful union picket was violently broken up by police. Union members were threatened, racially abused, beaten and arrested during a protest that turned into a violent confrontation after the aggressive intervention of the police. During the eighteen months between their indictments and their trial, when the felony charges were dismissed against the five men, they were required to wear electronic ankle bracelets and to observe a 7 *p.m.* to 7 *a.m.* curfew. Each of the five faced potential sentences of five years in prison. Front Line is concerned that their prosecution was a politically motivated attempt to intimidate labor rights activists and deny their right to freedom of association.

At 7 *p.m.* on January 19, 2000, the Danish container ship *Skodsborg* slipped into the port of Charleston, South Carolina, carrying a load of heavy machinery and bulk paper. The *Skodsborg*'s owners, the Nordana Corporation, had made arrangements with the Charleston Port Authority and Winia Stevedoring Incorporated for the ship to be unloaded by nonunion dockworkers. This would be the first time such a nonunion arrangement had been made in Charleston. If successful, other shipping companies would surely follow, breaking the back of organized labor in the port.

In response, Charleston Local 1422, a predominantly African American chapter of the International Longshoremen's Union, planned a peaceful protest for the time the ship was scheduled to dock. Such demonstrations had been a common occurrence in the port. The union and local police had maintained close, cordial relations, with police customarily assisting union members set up picket lines. One-hundred and fifty longshoremen (union dockworkers) planned to show up for the demonstration.

But South Carolina Attorney General Charlie Condon, the state's top law enforcement officer and an aspiring candidate for governor, decided to take the opportunity to demonstrate his commitment to a right-to-work (anti-union) environment.

Around 2 *p.m.* on January 19, over 600 law enforcement officers began massing at the port. The force included South Carolina State Troopers, agents of the South Carolina Law Enforcement Authority, Charleston police, and other police officers drawn from jurisdictions around the state.

The force was equipped with full riot gear: sidearm, shotguns, rubber bullets, tear gas canisters, concussion grenades, truncheons, helmets, and shields. Subpoenaed videotapes released subsequently showed the officers being prepared as if for a military battle. The force was accompanied by prison buses, dogs, armored personnel carriers, helicopters, and patrol boats. Police snipers took positions on nearby rooftops. Police cruisers surrounded the port. The union hall was encircled by police preventing ingress and egress. Local jails had been cleared of inmates to make room for the large number of arrests anticipated.

Union local President Ken Riley felt certain that the show of force was intended to provoke and escalate a confrontation. He called an emergency strategy meeting of union leaders. They decided on a course of action intended to avoid such a confrontation: the longshoremen would leave the dock and return at midnight, presumably after the police force had dispersed. But police informants at the meeting quickly relayed this strategy to the force.[53]

* * *

When the longshoremen returned to the port at midnight, the police presence was even larger. Police were lined up in military configurations as far as the longshoremen could see. The piers were lit up by klieg lights. Dockworker Leonard Riley, Ken's brother, recalls, "It looked like a scene from Vietnam or some war movie".

---

[53] Information on the Charleston 5 is derived from interviews conducted with members of the Local 1422 of the Longshoreman's Union, summer 2003.

The protesters were blocked off, harassed and intimidated, and prevented from taking up their usual positions. The police on the front lines began beating on their shields with batons. They shouted racial taunts and epithets at the predominantly African American demonstrators, including, "Bring it on, niggers! We're gonna bust your heads tonight". Officers began poking the demonstrators with batons.

Leonard Riley and others repeated over and over to police officers on the front line, "I need to go in there. I work in there". Riley and others tried to convince the demonstrators to remain under control. As a way of avoiding a pitched battle, he and fifteen to twenty other demonstrators moved down the pier's railroad tracks and made progress toward their usual work stations. Police pursued them with dogs. Leonard Riley was apprehended, smashed against a police cruiser, and handcuffed.

Meanwhile, back on the main line the confrontation became more volatile and more physical. Police began surging forward, swinging batons in wide arcs, felling demonstrators. The longshoremen fell back but police pursued them. More epithets were hurled by the police including, "Nigger, you better go back or we're gonna beat you", and "This nigger is fighting back!"

Gas canisters were fired. The demonstrators defended themselves and became increasingly physical.

Local 1422 president Ken Riley entered the fray and managed to separate the demonstrators from the police. But as he was persuading the last of the longshoreman to move, he was cracked in the back of the head by a police baton. He fell to the pavement, stunned and bleeding.

The longshoremen reacted to the felling of Riley by losing control and attacking the police line.

The confrontation lasted for one hour. Videos taken at the time showed the police firing rubber bullets and gas canisters, and wielding batons indiscriminately.

Eventually the demonstrators were pushed back to the union local hall. Nine longshoremen were arrested, including Leonard Riley. They were transported in prison buses, kneeling on the floor, handcuffed, heads forcibly bent down. A few of the prisoners vomited from trying to hold the position.

They spent the night in the Charleston city jail charged with misdemeanor trespass and were bonded out the following day.

But two days later, following the public intervention of Attorney General Condon, the nine longshoremen were re-arrested and charged with felony rioting, a charge carrying the possibility of five years in prison. Bond of $100,000 each was posted by family members.

A preliminary hearing was held thirty days later. After ten minutes consideration, a state court judge dismissed all the charges.

But Attorney General Condon persisted. He convened a grand jury and five of the longshoremen were indicted. They were charged with rioting, conspiracy to riot, and assaulting a police officer.

Condon assigned himself to prosecute the case and called for maximum bail, no plea bargain, and no leniency, promising "Jail, jail and more jail" and stating, "South Carolina is a strong right-to-work state, and a citizen's right not to join a union is absolute and will be fully protected".

* * *

The arrested longshoremen came to be known as the Charleston Five:

Elijah Ford, Jr., 40, has nearly a quarter century of service on the docks and for the past decade has been a foreman. He is responsible for overseeing the securing of various types of cargo on vessels and containers. "Nordana was a very stressful situation in which we had to protect our work jurisdiction, especially since the company responsible for stevedoring of the vessel is my main employer", he says.

Jason Edgerton, 23, has been an ILA member for three years. As a Clerk/Checker, he is responsible for checking cargoes scheduled to be off-loaded or on-loaded aboard vessels and preparing shipping/receiving paperwork in the various terminal yards. "I appreciate being part of an effort to defend our jobs", he says. "I think what we have done will help other dockworkers and ILA members in the future".

Kenneth Jefferson, 42, an ILA member for seven years, operates industrial equipment, such as fork lifts and yard hustlers. When the melee broke out that resulted in his arrest, Jefferson believes he was defending himself and his job. "When your livelihood is at stake, you have to take a stand."

Pete Washington, Jr., 48, is an all around dockworker and an ILA member for thirteen years. "Working people have to stand up for their rights", he says, "and if a similar situation to Nordana arises in the future, I would again protest to protect my union job".

Ricky Simmons, 38, a twenty-year ILA veteran, feels the union protest against Nordana's hiring of non-union labor was fruitful because since May the shipping line has resumed working with the union. "I'm proud of the fact we're once again working this vessel."

During the eighteen months between the indictments and their trial, the five men were confined to their homes from the hours of 7 *p.m.* to 7 *a.m.* They were required to wear electronic ankle bracelets that monitored their movements at all times. Each of the five faced potential sentences of five years in prison.

* * *

African American and labor rights activists and organizations protested the case, portraying it as emblematic of the treatment accorded black workers in the South.

The South Carolina American Federation of Labor – Congress of Industrial Organizations (AFL-CIO, the largest labor federation in the USA) formed a Campaign for Workers' Rights in South Carolina to build support for the five. The campaign was joined by Southern progressives and picked up by the national AFL-CIO and by dockworkers worldwide. In June 2001, 5000 people rallied in Charleston. The case became a focal point for defense of Black and union rights in the South. Many came to see a victory in the case as key to organizing a region historically known for endemic racism and opposition to unions.

Swedish Dockworkers' Union President Bjorn Borg, of the International Dockworkers' Council (IDC), announced that there would be a day of solidarity action on docks around the world. Longshoremen overseas threatened to close ports. As Ken Riley describes it,

> European dockers who heard about the struggle actually went aboard ships and handed letters to the captains of the vessels warning them that if they loaded in Charleston using workers other than the ILA, they wouldn't get unloaded [back in Europe]. After that began to happen, we did not have to contact Nordana. They contacted us and wanted to sit down and talk.

* * *

In the autumn of 2001, the court issued an order forbidding Attorney General Condon from speaking publicly about the case. But in October 2001, in comments to the press he compared the five longshoremen to the terrorists who had destroyed the World Trade Center on the previous September 11.

Pressure built from the public and government officials for Condon to be taken off the case. He finally removed himself and a new prosecutor was assigned. The house arrest of the five men was immediately lifted.

On November 11, 2001, the day the trial of the Charleston Five was scheduled to begin, all felony charges are dropped. Within days, a deal is reached on the misdemeanor trespass charges. The Five plead "no contest", and agree to pay a fine of $100 each.

* * *

The consequences of the demonstration and the ensuing confrontation have been dramatic for both the individuals and the institutions involved.

The Charleston Five returned to their jobs on the docks. While their job duties have remained the same, their experience has given them new commitment to union organizing.

Shortly after his release, Leonard Riley returned to work at the port. For four months after his release he was required to report on his whereabouts and seek special permission for travel. For six months he was prohibited from assembling on the dock or participating in demonstrations. He describes the current atmosphere in the port as much more tense and intimidating, with Port Authority police constantly patrolling and city police mounting a presence whenever ships come in.

To shield them from taunts and insults at school, Leonard Riley has tried to explain the position in which he found himself to his three children. He tells them how he had to "struggle for the right to make a living".

Following the blow from a police baton, Ken Riley's head wound required twelve stitches to be closed. Before the demonstration, Governor Jim Hodges had nominated Riley to a post on the Board of the State Port Authority. Afterward the South Carolina Chamber of Commerce and its member businesses mounted a campaign to prevent his appointment, fearing undue labor influence on the operation of the port. Eventually Governor Hodges succumbed to the pressure and rescinded the nomination. Although Riley has become even more active in state politics, the demonstration has precluded the possibility of formal governmental roles.

Twenty-seven longshoremen, including Ken Riley, were sued by Winia Stevedoring Incorporated for loss of income. In mediation a settlement was reached requiring the ILA to pay Winia $90,000.

In the primary election for Governor of South Carolina in 2002, Charlie Condon received less than ten percent of the vote. He currently holds no public office.

Governor Jim Hodges lost his bid for re-election in 2002.

The trials of the Charleston Five and the support they received from national and international labor and civil rights organizations resulted in a net gain for the labor movement in Charleston, in South Carolina, and in the southern United States. The position of Winia Stevedoring and similar non-union companies was significantly weakened. The International Longshoremen's Union primacy in the port was firmly established. A new coalition of labor unions, civil rights groups and community organizations has emerged.

* * *

Labor Rights, including the right to be a member of a trade union and to freedom of association, are guaranteed in international human rights standards and international labor standards. The United Nations Declaration on Human Rights Defenders includes in Article 5:

> For the purpose of promoting and protecting human rights and fundamental freedoms, everyone has the right, individually and in association with others... to meet or assemble peacefully... to form, join and participate in non-governmental organizations, associations or groups.

Ken Riley sees the situation this way:

> ILA Local 1422 is a predominately African American union and we are active in the community and in state politics. We are proof that working under a union contract can provide a living wage and that being organized means having political influence. That fact is what has scared those who want to maintain the old ways.

> Our deep sea local was formed in 1936. We have two white members. The clerks and checkers local, on the other hand, is all white. The first blacks are just now trying to make their way into that local. That's the way it's been throughout the history of the South, most of your southern ports were like this....it's not by accident, blacks were recruited to do the hard, back-breaking tasks on the waterfront.

> The attacks on us today are a direct result of our awakening to the fact that we do have responsibilities that extend beyond our membership, to their families, their community, and to our state. We are supposed to stay in our places. As long as we were being quiet and dormant, focusing only on our work, we were ok. But when you get involved, you are singled out in our state. Especially in a state where unions are not welcomed, where there's open hostility toward you. It's not a subtle thing,

it's not a hidden thing. When the Republican Party [of South Carolina] can announce that the two top items on their agenda for the year 2000 was number one, education, and number two, to rid the state of labor unions and union influence in state government, you know it's open season. It's not something you have to wonder about.

South Carolina is like a Third World country for working people. That's actually the way we're being marketed. We have some of the most productive workers in the world, paid twenty percent less than the national average. There is a hostile climate toward unions: South Carolina has the lowest union density in all fifty states, except North Carolina.

Bill Fletcher of the AFL-CIO, says,

When we look at the case of the Charleston Five, we have to look beyond the individuals and the local union....The conviction of the Charleston Five could [have] inspire[d] a wave of sentiment on the part of government authorities and employers that this kind of massive repression is acceptable and more importantly, that they can get away with it.

Business in South Carolina and the politicians who support it are even proposing to give people the ability to file harassment charges against union organizers. Think about the chilling effect this will have, not just on paid union organizers, but on volunteer and rank-and-file members participating in union organizing drives. Workers will have to stop and think, 'Am I going to be sued by someone if I go to someone's door to talk to them about the union, and I come across someone manipulated by the company into making these charges?'

This is something we see in the US time and time again. When capital wants to implement certain changes, they often go after people of color first. They hope they'll frame the issue in such a way that whites will decide that the issue is irrelevant to them. ILA 1422 is a largely African American local. Moving against them is a way of introducing a very definite change for the worse in the whole community, for labor-capital relations in general in South Carolina. This is a direct attack on the freedom of association. It's a direct attack on the right of workers to peacefully protest. It's a direct attack on the right of workers to organize.

Ken Riley concludes,

> Sometimes something has to happen like this for everyone to wake up and realize it is time to get together. It's been a tough time waking people up, but I think it's starting to happen. Sometimes things happen and you don't recognize right away what this is going to mean. Certainly we didn't think it would have meant all of this when we were out there that night getting our heads bashed in. But it didn't take long to realize the community was there.

Lynne Stewart
New York City

"Never deny the politics; that's your shield and your sword. Tell the truth on the charges, but embrace the politics" – Lynne Stewart

Anti-terrorism legislation and practices in the wake of the September 11, 2001, attacks on the World Trade Center and the Pentagon have made human rights defenders in the United States increasingly vulnerable to repressive consequences, especially defense attorneys with a commitment to protecting civil liberties. The Department of Justice and its constituent entities such as the Federal Bureau of Investigation (FBI) and the Immigration and Naturalization Service (INS) increasingly monitor and intervene in situations that allegedly impact US "national security". – Such action has had a chilling effect on human rights defenders who stand between government agencies and potential victims of abuses.

The case of Lynne Stewart demonstrates that defenders of "terrorist" suspects may, by virtue of their defense activities, become suspects themselves.

Lynne Stewart, a sixty-three-year-old civil liberties attorney practicing in New York City, has built an illustrious career defending those alleged to be revolutionaries, terrorists, and others perceived as threats by the US Government. Most recently, Stewart has provided legal representation for Sheik Omar Ali Abdel Rahman, who was convicted in 1995 of plotting terrorism against the United States, including planning to bomb landmarks in New York. As a result of her defense of Sheik Abdel Rahman, Stewart herself has been charged by the US Department of Justice with providing "material support" to a terrorist organization.

Stewart and her colleagues have steadfastly and unequivocally maintained her innocence. They point out that the charges leveled by the Government accuse her of doing what any good lawyer would do in defense of a client.[54]

* * *

---

[54] Material for this section is based on interviews with Lynne Stewart, Ralph Poynter, and others involved in her case.

Despite her history of civil libertarian activism and her understanding of the workings of the federal judiciary, Stewart says she had no inkling that she was the subject of a three-year investigation by the Department of Justice until the morning of April 9, 2002, when Federal agents arrested her at her New York home. Stewart recalls that she was upstairs preparing to go to court when she hears her husband downstairs speaking to a group of law enforcement agents. He says he wants to see their warrant and identification. Stewart assumes that because of her husband's lifelong political involvement, the agents are there to arrest him. She reassures him, "Don't worry, we'll have you out by lunch". Whereupon one of the agents says, "We're not here for him, we're here for you".

Stewart remembers being astounded. She is handcuffed and taken to FBI headquarters in Manhattan. At the same time, FBI agents enter Stewart's office and search it until 6 *p.m.* They remove computer hard-drives, address books, appointment books, and rolodex files of clients. After three hours at FBI headquarters, Stewart is taken across the street and locked up at US District Court for the southern district of New York.

Stewart's own lawyer, Susan Tipograph, brings the indictment to her cell. Stewart has been indicted under the 1996 Antiterrorism Act and charged with four counts of aiding and abetting a terrorist organization, charges that carry the potential for forty years in prison. The indictment indicates that Stewart's communications with Sheik Abdel Rahman had been the subject of government wiretaps for more than two years, probably by means of Foreign Intelligence Surveillance Act warrants that do not require probable cause, but only a suspicion that one is engaging in terrorist activities.

The indictment outlines four charges against Stewart: providing material support to a terrorist organization; conspiracy to provide material support to a terrorist organization; defrauding the United States Government; and lying to the United States Government. The first two charges are felonies, each one carrying a maximum sentence of fifteen years in prison. The latter two carry maximum sentences of five years each.

Stewart is released after her children sign a bond for $500,000.

Against the advice of attorneys and friends, at 5 *p.m.* on the day of her arrest Stewart holds a press conference that draws coverage from media outlets across New York and the country. She takes the opportunity to deny categorically all the charges. She questions the intrusive methods used by the government in gathering information for the indictment and suggests that her long history of political activism may have had more than a little to do with her arrest.

On the morning Lynne Stewart was arrested, United States Attorney General John Ashcroft arrives in New York City. That evening, in front of national and international television outlets, he announces criminal indictments against four defendants, including Lynne Stewart. He states,

> Since our country was attacked over six months ago, I have sought to reassure the American people that the actions of the Department of Justice are carefully designed to target terrorists and to protect American rights and freedoms. Today's actions pursue the same objectives with the same protections in mind. We will not look the other way when our institutions of justice are subverted. We will not ignore those who claim rights for themselves while they seek their destruction for others. We will, in the President's words, defend freedom—and justice—no matter what the cost.[55]

Later that evening, Ashcroft appears on "Late Nite With David Letterman", a television program watched by tens of millions of American households. He sings his own composition, "Screaming Eagles". He announces Stewart's arrest as a significant development in the fight against terror.

Stewart secures the legal representation of Michael Tigar, a prominent professor of constitutional law at American University and a renowned civil rights defense attorney. At her arraignment, dozens of defense attorneys are in the courtroom—not only eager to offer her support, but also apprehensive that the Justice Department's aggressive war on terrorism might include monitoring *their* conversations with particularly controversial clients.

---

[55] http://www.cnn.com/TRANSCRIPTS/0204/09/bn.03.html

As a result of the charges, Stewart's law practice suffers a dramatic decline. Much of her income has come from her selection to represent indigent clients under the Criminal Justice Act. For indigent persons accused of a crime, the US Criminal Justice Act provides attorneys' fees. Attorneys are chosen to represent those individuals by the relevant court. Such clients charged with Federal offenses formed the greater part of Stewart's income. She is now barred from being selected for that work.

Tigar and Stewart win an early procedural victory when the judge appointed a "Special Master" – a lawyer outside the Department of Justice – to determine which records seized from Stewart's office could be examined by the Government. Stewart also wins the right to visit clients in Federal prisons, but she is barred from contact with Sheik Abdel Rahman.

Oral arguments in Stewart's case are presented in mid-June, 2003, in a United States federal courtroom in New York City. On June 13 presiding Judge John G. Koeltl questions government prosecutor Christopher J. Morvillo on the distinction between political activity protected by the US Constitution and criminal conduct in terrorism cases. The prosecutor replies, "You know it when you see it, your honor".

On July 22 Stewart receives Judge Koeltl's seventy-seven page decision. She is acquitted of the two charges related to providing material support to terrorists. The decision concludes that government prosecutors had applied the 1996 Anti-Terrorism Act in a way that was unconstitutionally vague. The judge did not attempt to strike down the entire 1996 anti-terrorism law, but he said the defendants were correct to argue against a prosecution based solely on use of telephones and other means of communication.

Trial on the charges of lying to the Government and defrauding the Government is scheduled for January 10, 2004. A conviction on any of these charges would result in a prison sentence and the loss of Stewart's license to practice law.

The court's decision in Stewart's case has a broader impact. It protects defense attorneys from being charged under the 1996 law for providing "material support". In Stewart's words, "The Government cannot indict a lawyer for doing what lawyers do, and then claim that that is materially aiding a terrorist organization". The decision also affirms the validity of

First Amendment defenses in response to charges brought under the 1996 law.

Michael Tigar says of the decision,

> The ruling holds that the First Amendment of the United States Constitution, freedom of speech, press, association, and petition, requires that if you're going to limit speech, you have to do so with statutes that let people know what they can and cannot say or do. And that this statute as applied by these prosecutors, flunks that test. I think the significant thing is that the defense of Lynne Stewart has always been a defense of the right to defend, the right to counsel, and, of course, if you empower brave lawyers like Lynne Stewart, you help people. But this opinion goes broader than that. It says that the prosecution is an attack on the right of all people to express themselves. And that means that the judge has taken a view of the First Amendment that empowers, not just lawyers to defend people, but all people who want to talk about, to protest and analyze the current American policy in the Middle East. It means that lawyers who give their services to represent people accused of terrorist crimes—so-called terrorist crimes, can breathe a little easier if this opinion holds up. This case was, from the beginning, an attempt to chill the exercise of vigorous advocacies. So let's hope that some more lawyers take courage....[56]

The judge's decision was a significant setback for the US Government's judicial strategy of suppressing suspected terrorists. Nearly all criminal terrorism cases brought by the US Government since September 11, 2001, have depended upon the 1996 law, the Anti-Terrorism Act. The law had been used successfully against Lyman Farris, charged with plotting to blow up the Brooklyn Bridge; Sami Al-Arian, accused of providing financial support to alleged Palestinian terrorists; John Walker Lindh, an American who fought with the Taliban in Afghanistan; and alleged terrorist sympathizers (so-called "sleeper-cell" members) in New York state, Seattle, Detroit, and Portland, Oregon.

---

[56] http://lists.indymedia.org/pipermail/imc-nyc-print/2003-July/008689.html

The Act criminalizes the provision of assistance to foreign organizations identified as terrorist on a list maintained by the US Department of State. In addition to weapons, explosives and money, communications equipment, personnel, and training are also identified as "material support". In allegedly passing on messages from her client, the Government argued that Stewart provided communication equipment and personnel in the form of her telephone and herself. It was this application of this law that was rejected by Judge Koeltl in Lynne Stewart's case.

David Cole, a professor of law at Georgetown University in Washington, DC, has said, "There is a reason that this statute has been a linchpin in the post-9/11 war on terror. It does not require the government to prove any actual connection to terrorist conduct but instead allows it to rely on guilt by association".

Eric M. Freedman, a law professor at Hofstra University, says, "The government's position that one can be locked up for decades for expressions of political positions on the telephone amounts to simple thought control".

Nevertheless, four months after Judge Koeltl's decision, Attorney General Ashcroft and US Attorney James Comey announced a reframed indictment that attaches different material to the original charges. Stewart must again face a potential sentence of forty years in prison.

There has been much speculation about why Stewart was targeted for prosecution by the Department of Justice when many other attorneys were engaged in similar activities. Some have suggested that Attorney General Ashcroft may have seen Stewart as an easy target because she is a woman, a 1960s-era activist, and a prominent civil libertarian. Stewart herself believes that her arrest was a political decision. She doubts that New York District prosecutors would have brought a case against her without pressure from the Department of Justice. Says Stewart, "You make choices. You live your life in a certain way and you know there could be consequences, especially when you've been fighting the Government as long as I have".

The United Nations Declaration on Human Rights Defenders states in Article 9 that everyone has the right "to offer and provide professionally qualified legal assistance or other relevant advice and assistance in defending human rights and fundamental freedoms". Article 12 states

> The State shall take all necessary measures to ensure the protection by the competent authorities of everyone, individually and in association with others, against any violence, threats, retaliation, *de facto* or *de jure* adverse discrimination, pressure or any other arbitrary action as a consequence of his or her legitimate exercise of the rights referred to in the present Declaration.

* * *

Lynne Stewart grew up in Queens, a suburb of New York City. In 1957, she entered a strict Calvinist college in Michigan, where she encountered severe restrictions on behavior, especially for women. She also witnessed appalling treatment of Mexican migrant agricultural workers. She transferred to American University in Washington DC, and completed her studies at Wagner College on New York's Staten Island.

In 1962 she took a job as a librarian at an elementary school in Harlem, a predominately African American section of New York City, where she became aware of how deep and profound the effects of racism in the USA could be. She says, "What made me become radical? Harlem, 1962".

It was also at this time that she met her lifelong partner, the New York education activist Ralph Poynter. Together they worked for community control of schools in African American neighborhoods in New York City. For his participation in related demonstrations, Poynter was arrested several times and lost his teaching license.

The surveillance, infiltration, and eventually successful co-opting of the movement for local control of New York City schools were a priority for the US Department of Justice. Because Stewart belonged to groups that had been infiltrated by government informants, she has appeared in Department of Justice surveillance files from the early 1960s.

In the mid-1960s Stewart moved to a working class neighborhood on the lower east side of Manhattan, where she would continue to reside for thirty-five years. In the early 1970s she graduated from the law school at Rutgers University in New Jersey. At the same time, she and Ralph were raising seven children and operating a motorcycle repair shop. During this period she was arrested several times for her participation in protests against US military involvement in Vietnam.

Within two years of graduating from law school, she had her own practice, writing wills, defending misdemeanor charges, representing residents of Chinatown and those charged with offenses related to their sexual identity, and as she says, "Everything that came in the door".

In 1981 Stewart began to combine her law experience with her political concerns. That year several of her friends were arrested at JFK Airport for protesting the arrival of the South African national rugby team. Objecting to the team's presence in the US was a significant action for anti-apartheid activists.

The same year members of the radical Black Liberation Army and the Weather Underground killed two policemen while robbing an armored car in Nyack, New York. Stewart decided to represent two of the defendants. One client was acquitted; the other's guilt was never in question. Stewart used the opportunity of her defense to elucidate the elements of US politics and society that the radical groups felt compelled to attack.

Through this and later cases, Stewart's philosophical and practical approach was, "Never deny the politics; that's your shield and your sword. Tell the truth on the charges, but embrace the politics". Presenting the political context in which alleged offenses were committed became Stewart's key legal strategy. This is often made more palatable to a general audience by her plain and direct way of speaking. She is renowned for her brilliant, straightforward, often blunt trial summations.

In 1988 Stewart served as lead counsel with William Kunstler in the defense of a young black man named Larry Davis. Allegedly acting on a warrant that was never found, thirty-six policemen arrived at Davis' house to arrest him. In the subsequent shoot-out, six police officers were wounded. Stewart proved through forensic evidence that the police fired first and won an acquittal for Davis by reason of self-defense.

In 1989 Stewart refused to testify before a grand jury against one of her own clients and was charged with contempt. She spent part of her time over the next ten years in and out of appellate courts defending the right of lawyers to refuse to divulge information on their clients.

* * *

In late 1994 Stewart was persuaded by former US Attorney General Ramsey Clark to take on the case of Sheik Abdel Rahman, who stood accused of planning terror attacks on New York City landmarks, including the United Nations building, the George Washington Bridge, the Holland Tunnel, and the FBI building. Sheik Abdel Rahman was charged with "seditious conspiracy", a rarely invoked charge intended to prevent violent overthrow of the US Government. He was also charged with plotting to murder Egyptian President Hosni Mubarak.

Stewart and Sheik Abdel Rahman interviewed each other at his place of detention, the Metropolitan Correctional Center in Manhattan; they agreed that she would be the right person to defend him. Stewart says, "I was convinced then and remain convinced that Sheik Abdel Rahman was wrongfully charged and wrongfully convicted, and was the victim of the long reach of President Mubarak and the Government of Egypt". She believes that Sheik Abdel Rahman's arrest and prosecution can only be understood in the context of the importance of Egypt to US policy in the Middle East.

Stewart found herself with two months to prepare her defense while the US Government had been preparing its prosecution for two years. But Stewart regarded the Government's case as built on a fundamental weakness: the comments made by Sheik Abdel Rahman on which the charges were based had been solicited and drawn from him by a government informer.

Stewart is clear that Sheik Abdel Rahman may well understand and to some degree share the motivations for planning terrorist bombings against the USA. But that does not mean he would participate in planning such attacks, let alone assist in carrying them out. Stewart describes Sheik Abdel Rahman as "sustained by his religious and political beliefs, which are inseparable. He is very intelligent, very charming and burns very bright with his convictions of how change should come about".

Sheik Abdel Rahman's position as a designated Muslim religious leader places him in a position to be sought out for his advice, which he feels compelled by his faith to give freely. At a very young age, his parents placed him in the care of religious leaders at an Egyptian mosque renowned for its teaching. Blind from the age of two, he had memorized the Koran by the age of ten. He was destined to become, and in fact became, a venerated religious elder. He does not speak English.

However, Michael Mukazy, the presiding judge in Sheik Abdel Rahman's trial refused to allow a defense based on the Sheik's religious responsibilities in spite of the fact that the charges were based on evidence from a government informer who approached Sheik Abdel Rahman asking for spiritual guidance. He also denied Stewart's request to provide education on Islam to the jury, on the basis that the witnesses called in that effort would, "confuse the jury".

Sheik Abdel Rahman was convicted in October 1995, and immediately airlifted to the federal prison hospital in Springfield, Missouri.

An appeal was made to a three-judge panel at the Second Circuit US Court in Manhattan. The decision, pending for a year after the close of arguments, affirmed the conviction in language that effectively blocked further defense options.

In June of 1996 the Bureau of Prisons used its Special Administrative Measures to further isolate Sheik Abdel Rahman. He was permitted no visitors other than blood relations, all of whom are in Egypt and cannot get visas; over the course of ten years, he has had one visit from his wife. His phone calls were limited to one per month to his wife and one per week to his lawyers. Because he is always held in isolation, he is not allowed to attend religious services although he can worship in his cell. He is not allowed contact with the press, and all his mail, in the form of audiotapes and Braille, is vetted by the FBI.

In order to maintain any contact with her client, Stewart and the other defense attorneys signed an agreement to abide by these strictures of the Special Administrative Measures.

As a result of Stewart's efforts, Sheik Abdel Rahman was moved in the autumn of 1996 to Rochester, Minnesota, where his prison medical care improved and he had access to the Mayo Clinics. As his diabetes has worsened, he became largely unable to care for himself. Furthermore Stewart became increasingly concerned about the effects of isolation on his mental health.

In spite of the restrictions of the Special Administrative Measures, in June 2000 Sheik Abdel Rahman wrote a public letter to an attorney in Egypt representing imprisoned members of the violent opposition group Gamma Islamya, to which he had been spiritual advisor. In 1997, Gamma Islamya had signed a cease-fire with the Mubarak Government that has held until the present day.

In the letter, Sheik Abdel Rahman made the following points. While Gamma Islamya had observed a cease-fire for three years, no concessions had been forthcoming from the Egyptian Government. There had been no releases of the organization's members who were detained without charge. Military trials were continuing; torture was being used. While he acknowledged that he was not on the scene and not fully informed, he nevertheless questioned whether the cease-fire should continue.

The substance of this letter was made public in a press release issued only to Reuters in Cairo, and its text was eventually carried only in the Cairo press. But the person reading the text over the phone to the Reuters reporter was Lynne Stewart. Soon after, Stewart received a call from Patrick Fitzgerald, Assistant US Attorney for southern New York, who berated her for reading the statement to Reuters.

In January 2001, after the negotiations with the Government, Stewart received a new set of Special Administrative Measures that allowed her to visit Sheik Abdel Rahman. Months later, Stewart learned that in the interval the Department of Justice, acting under the Foreign Intelligence Surveillance Act, had placed cameras and recording devices in the area where her visits took place. A recording device was also placed in the phone Sheik Abdel Rahman used to call Stewart and his other attorneys.

* * *

On September 11, 2001, Lynne Stewart was driving to work in Manhattan when her son phoned her to say he has seen black smoke rising from the towers of the World Trade Center. She turns on her car radio, heard of a second plane hitting the towers and knows immediately it is a terrorist attack. The World Trade Center is ten blocks from her office; she is acquainted with some of those who die in the building. She has the same response of shock, horror, and outrage felt by other New Yorkers.

In the wake of the attacks, Sheik Abdel Rahman was transferred to a special wing of the Federal prison in Florence, Colorado. Stewart has not been allowed to see him since their last visit in July of 2001. But she is still suing to improve the conditions of his imprisonment, which have included inadequate medical care, routine flooding in the cell, lack of Arabic speaking staff, delayed response to his calls for a guard. In addition to his blindness and acute diabetes, he also suffers from heart disease.

Sheik Abdel Rahman continues to serve a prison sentence of life plus sixty-five years in Florence, Colorado.

Lynne Stewart faces the new charges of "providing material support" to terrorists in a trial that is scheduled to begin in May, 2004.

The United Nations Declaration on Human Rights Defenders states in Article 9 that everyone has the right "to offer and provide professionally qualified legal assistance or other relevant advice and assistance in defending human rights and fundamental freedoms". Article 12 states

> The State shall take all necessary measures to ensure the protection by the competent authorities of everyone, individually and in association with others, against any violence, threats, retaliation, *de facto* or *de jure* adverse discrimination, pressure or any other arbitrary action as a consequence of his or her legitimate exercise of the rights referred to in the present Declaration.

Charles Tisdale
Jackson, Mississippi

"The attacks made me decide to stay. Would have moved to Memphis if they'd left me alone"—Charles Tisdale

On July 1, 1978, Charles Tisdale became the owner and publisher of the *Jackson Advocate* of Jackson, Mississippi. Just two weeks passed before he received the first threat on his life; the most recent such threat came in November of 2003. Between these dates, Tisdale has received hundreds of threats. He and his staff have been routinely harassed and intimidated, both by local authorities and by racists. Attempts have been made to burn down his home. The *Advocate*'s offices have been burglarized and shot to pieces.

On January 23, 1998, Tisdale received an anonymous phone call threatening his life. He complained to reporters that city and state authorities had ignored his previous reports of threats, vandalism, and drive-by shootings. Three nights later the offices of the *Advocate* were completely gutted by a firebomb

The day following the bombing, *Advocate* staff members began producing the newspaper from Tisdale's home.

* * *

The city of Jackson, originally designed along rationalist Enlightenment principles by Thomas Jefferson, is the capital and largest city of Mississippi. Its population of 185,000 is seventy-three percent African American. Of Mississippi's 2.5 million people, forty percent are African American, the largest percentage of any state in the USA. The state's African American underclass is the poorest in the USA. Per capita income in Jackson is $17,116; twenty-three percent of families are below the poverty line.

In the 1960s Jackson was a prominent battleground in the civil rights struggle. Enormous pressure, including a boycott of businesses, was required to force integration of facilities and services. Police unleashed attack dogs and water cannons on demonstrators. In 1961 a bus full of Freedom Riders were arrested and charged with "disturbing the peace". Local National

Association for the Advancement of Colored People (NAACP) leader and national spokesperson Medgar Evers was killed at his home in Jackson by a white supremacist.[57]

Four decades later, despite much progress, systemic racism persists in more covert modes. In the late 1990s depressed downtown areas in Jackson and many other urban areas in the USA were being developed for a middle class that had once fled inner-city conditions but had now grown tired of commuting and wanted to return to the amenities of city life. Such development nearly always displaced poor people, both white and minorities, who had remained in the downtowns. And unlike middle class whites, these displaced poor did not have the luxury of moving to the suburbs.

* * *

Charles Tisdale was born in rural Athens, Alabama on November 7, 1926, one of a family of seventeen children. His father worked the land until the farm was lost in the Great Depression of the 1930s; thereafter he supported his family through day jobs and yard work. Tisdale remembers him as a poet and songwriter, an intellectual who read three newspapers every day.

Tisdale's mother was "a stern and courageous woman", who insisted that her children stand up for their rights. She was a fierce defender of the family who "would shoot in a minute". In her last letter to Tisdale, she said, "Please send me a new pistol as mine is rusty".

From the time he was 15, Tisdale worked the migrant circuit of tobacco farms, especially in Connecticut. However, at 18 he was able to enter college in Memphis, Tennessee, and began working at the *Memphis World* newspaper.

Between 1950 and 1975 Tisdale worked for a number of African American newspapers in Chicago, New York City, and Huntsville, Alabama. In these years he also became a committed civil rights activist. In 1965 he was jailed in Memphis for participating in civil rights demonstrations. He organized for

---

[57] Unless otherwise cited, information on Charles Tisdale was gathered from interviews conducted by the author with him and other residents of Jackson, Mississippi, in November 2003, and January 2004.

the civil rights movement in Mississippi with Martin Luther King and was in Memphis when King was assassinated there.

In 1978 the widow of Percy Greene, the owner of *the Jackson Advocate*, persuaded Tisdale to run the paper. He moved to Jackson and purchased the *Advocate* in July of 1978.

* * *

The *Jackson Advocate* is the oldest African American newspaper in Mississippi and the largest weekly in the state. Its total circulation is 20,000, but only 7400 of that number are in the Jackson area; many subscribers reside in major US and European cities. The paper's motto is from Robert Burns: "A man's a man for all that".

The *Advocate* has an editorial policy of promoting civil rights and fighting discrimination. Tisdale says, "I think newspapers that provide information are the most essential tool in a democracy. I always wanted to have my say. This is true liberty, when free men speak freely".

In 1927 Percy Greene founded the *Colored Veteran*, a newspaper that campaigned for the rights of African American veterans returning from World War I. The paper provided information about government benefits that were being distributed almost exclusively to white veterans. In 1937 Greene suspended publication but resumed the next year under the banner of the *Jackson Advocate*. In 1940 Greene and thirty other publishers formed a consortium of African American newspapers to bring relevant information to Black readers in the USA. That association led to the Negro Newspaper Publishers Association, which promoted coverage of injustices against and accomplishments by African Americans.[58]

Jackson Advocate reporter and historian Barbara Harris reflects, "This is where the *Jackson Advocate*'s purpose deviates from traditional media. Though it is a newspaper of general circulation, published primarily for the benefit of everyone, its content is of particular interest to African Americans and others who follow human and civil rights very closely".[59]

---

[58] Barbara Harris, 'Six and One-Half Decades of Struggle Continues', *Jackson Advocate*, 18 September 2003.
[59] Ibid.

The *Advocate* has won over fifty local and national awards for public service journalism, including the City of Jackson Community Service Award, the Mississippi Legislative Black Caucus Award for Excellence, the Southern Christian Leadership Council Journalism Award, and the National Black Chamber of Commerce Newspaper of the Year.

In 1988 the US magazine *Newsday* referred to the *Advocate* as a "national treasure". In 1989, the Dutch magazine *El Siviar* and Germany's *Der Speigel* called attention to the *Advocate's* record of accomplishment. In 1991, the National Newspaper Publisher's Association named the *Advocate* the third-best African American newspaper in the USA. The National Alliance of Third World Journalists has chosen Tisdale and the *Advocate* for their Jose Marti Journalist of Struggle Award.

Mississippi's leading university paper said this:

> A newspaper, especially the one that serves Jackson's sizeable Black population, is a community lifeline whose importance goes beyond a mere business.... The *Advocate* and its publisher have been suffering from hate crime too often and for too long. The recent break-ins suggest that Mississippi is not as close o the goal of social harmony as we would like to think. Freedom of speech is our most precious right, yet there are some who cannot stand the idea of a black person exercising that right.[60]

* * *

Under Tisdale's leadership, the *Jackson Advocate* has taken provocative editorial positions and provided aggressive coverage of human rights abuses, civil rights violations, job discrimination, and political malfeasance.

Strongly pro-union, the *Advocate* in the 1980s took on Warren Hood, one of Jackson's leading power brokers in an eight-year campaign supporting the right of workers at Hood Furniture to a union of their own choice. The paper has also consistently backed Jackson's municipal workers' unions in their still-ongoing struggle for recognition.

---

[60] *Daily Mississippian*, 8 June 2000.

Tisdale and the *Advocate* were among the early and persistent voices demanding a new trial for the murderer of civil right activist Medgar Evers. Evers' efforts in the early 1960s to integrate stores and services in Jackson included a boycott of businesses and the admission of the first Black student to the University of Mississippi. He became a figure of national importance, lionized by Black leaders and reviled by Southern whites.

On June 12, 1963, Evers was shot to death in the driveway of his home. The accused killer, white supremacist Byron De La Beckwith, stood trial twice in the 1960s, but in both cases the all-white juries could not reach a verdict. Finally, with the pressure of Tisdale and the *Advocate*, a third trial was held in 1994. Beckwith was convicted and sentenced to life in prison.

Mississippi jails and prisons are plagued by the deaths by hanging of young Black men in police custody. Almost all are officially reported as suicides. The *Advocate* and independent investigators believe them to be deliberate lynchings by prison staff or by white inmates in acts condoned by guards. Tisdale's interviews with coroners have led him to the conclusion that the methods of hanging, such as on a doorknob, are inconsistent with "unsupervised suicide".

In March of 1998 the *Advocate* reported on secret files of a Mississippi state segregation-era spy agency. The documents clearly demonstrated the efforts of state government and law enforcement officials, often with the collusion of the Federal Bureau of investigation (FBI), to discredit the civil rights movement and prevent integration of schools.[61]

Advocate articles and editorials had been strongly critical of some of Jackson's rising African American leadership, including Mayor Harvey Johnson and former City Council President Louis Armstrong. Armstrong has been the subject of articles and editorials in the *Advocate* questioning his business dealings, including colluding with contractors to make it difficult for fellow African Americans to get jobs.

In 2002 the *Advocate* charged the Mississippi Attorney General with illegally reallocating $20 million from the Tobacco Trust, a fund formed

---

[61] *New Media*, June 1999.

with assets from state health suits against tobacco companies. And the paper has for twelve years reported on illegal activities of the Jackson County District Attorney's office, including the surveillance and monitoring of suspected political dissidents.

Recently the *Advocate* came to the defense of a white woman in Jackson who was harassed and fired from her job for dating a Black man. The man was subsequently shot to death on October 11, 2003.[62]

But perhaps no story the *Advocate* has pursued has so unnerved its subjects as his ongoing battle with Jackson's Capital Center Improvement Group (CCI), which Tisdale calls "a group of wealthy, powerful, and essentially white business owners supported by government officials". From 1995 to the present, Tisdale has relentlessly uncovered corruption and malfeasance in the connections between CCI and local government.

In the 1990s CCI had established a "downtown improvement district", a zone in which businesses would control access, beautification, security. Creation of the district was put to a public vote and rejected. CCI changed the language of their proposal and arranged a second vote; this time it passed. The American Civil Liberties Union and the Southern Christian Leadership Conference have filed a suit against the city contending that the second election was illegal.[63]

Tisdale ran stories charging that CCI improperly received large amounts of money from the city and suggesting that local business leaders had targeted downtown Jackson for gentrification, planning to make it impossible for poor African Americans to remain there. Tisdale says "As soon as they get rid of us, whites will return because it has become too expensive and too inconvenient to drive from the suburbs".

Facing a $30 million lawsuit brought by Tisdale, the CCI attempted to change its image by changing its name to the Downtown Jackson Partners Incorporated. But Tisdale maintains that substantively nothing has changed, the suit is pending, and the *Advocate* continues to pursue the story.

---

[62] *Atlanta Journal Constitution*, 12 October 2003.

[63] Ibid.

Since Tisdale took over in 1978, the *Advocate* has been the target of twenty-one violent attacks. Almost immediately he experienced a series of dozens of break-ins at the paper, including sixteen in one month in 1982.

Tisdale says,

> The *Advocate* had a history of being an "accommodationist" newspaper. It was presumed that that character of the paper would remain. The *Advocate*, under Percy Greene, had formed an alliance where they would [publish] conservative views to please white folks. When that alliance was no longer possible, the Advocate became viewed as a hostile element. The FBI, the Internal Revenue Service (IRS), the State Tax Commission, Department of Economic Development, and the Mississippi Employment Security Commission, attacked us.

When Jackson's traditional economic investors questioned Tisdale about his plans for the paper, he would only say that his intent was, "To run a free newspaper in a free society". This independent attitude caused the *Advocate*'s advertising income to plummet. Longtime white clients such as Mississippi Power and Light and Deposit Guaranty National Bank withdrew their ads.[64]

The first violent attack on the *Jackson Advocate* came on the night of December 19, 1981. Windows and offices were riddled with gunfire and the building was firebombed. Less than a month later, on January 16, 1982, two members of the Ku Klux Klan fired over 3000 rounds of ammunition into the offices. When the Klansmen were arrested, they were found in possession of a submachine gun and 30,000 rounds of ammunition. The District Attorney refused at first to prosecute until forced to do so by pressure from the African American community. The two men admitted to making the attack because the *Advocate* had been critical of some of their "associates". They were tried, found guilty, and sentenced; one received ten

---

[64] Harris.

132

years in prison, the other three years. Neither served more than eight months.[65]

Throughout the 1980s and 1990s, the *Advocate* endured untold number of acts of vandalism, robberies, threats, and political and economic attacks. Law enforcement officials harassed *Advocate* employees, denying them access to news scenes and stories and publicly referring to reporter Barbara Harris as a "black bitch".

Employees of the *Advocate* allege that The Chamber of Commerce discouraged businesses from advertising in the paper and city administrators pressured and harassed the paper by interrupting power and water service, and by bribing *Advocate* employees not to investigate certain stories or to leave the paper altogether.

Tisdale's wife Alice, who now manages the *Advocate*, has been arrested and jailed for minor traffic infractions. The sidewalk boxes selling the *Advocate* are routinely stolen or destroyed, even at sites near police stations – something that does not happen to other newspapers.

In May of 1995, just prior to a hearing on Tisdale's criminal suit against a Jackson City Councilman, he was arrested for assault as a result of a public argument with his attorney. Tisdale says he has since learned that the arrest was ordered by the mayor and the city councilman in order to tarnish Tisdale's image.

One shooting at Tisdale's home in the summer of 1997 caused his 11-year old daughter to hide under the bed for many nights.

Just after midnight on January 26, 1998, the doors of the *Advocate* offices were kicked in, files were strewn on the floor, furniture and papers were doused with gasoline, and two homemade Molotov cocktails were thrown through the windows of the *Advocate* offices. The resulting fire gutted the interior of the *Advocate*. Insurance estimates of the damage amounted to $100,000, but because the *Advocate*'s library of old, rare, irreplaceable books was destroyed, Barbara Harris guesses that total damages amount to around two million dollars.

---

[65] Ibid.

Although security video cameras mounted on the adjacent Federal Building captured the incident, the key tape conveniently disappeared. Local law enforcement authorities, including the arson investigator, were unable to identify any suspects.

In 1999 Clinton Moses, who stood convicted of two armed bank robberies but had not yet been sentenced, confessed to the bombing. He claimed Louis Armstrong had paid him to do so because he was angered by the *Advocate's* coverage of his political and economic dealings. Apparently in return for his guilty plea, Moses received a sentence of ten years in prison for the bombing, and sentencing on the robbery charges was waived. Moses is scheduled to be released in early 2005.

Tisdale and many of his associates have never accepted Moses' version of the attack. While they have no doubt that Moses carried out the bombing, they do not believe Armstrong arranged it. Instead, they assume that investors within the CCI or members of their private policing unit were responsible.

Tisdale says of his relationship with Armstrong, "We'd been warring for twenty-seven years and for twenty-seven years every time one of us made the other one angry we'd rent a hotel room and have a fistfight. We'd had a fistfight just before the bombing and he beat the **** out of me. So there was no reason for him to do it".

Stephanie Parker Weaver, Mississippi Executive Secretary of Southern Christian Leadership Conference (SCLC) argued, "The *Jackson Advocate* was firebombed for one reason and one reason only. It has spoken 'truth to power' for many, many years—Black truth to white power". She called it "a hate crime of the highest order". Alice Tisdale said at the time, "It's like times past, but they're back again. People are supposed to have moved past that".[66]

Mississippi's sole Black Congressman, Bennie Thompson, finally convinced the FBI and the Department of Alcohol, Tobacco, and Firearms (ATF) to investigate the bombing, but after three months neither agency had

---

[66] Gina Holland, Associated Press, 27 January 1998

interviewed Charles Tisdale. Thompson held a hearing at the state capital in Jackson to explore the reasons why no investigation had been made. The FBI said it was investigating, but had no suspects and no plans to make arrests. Local government staff and FBI agents dropped hints that Tisdale himself was responsible for the bombing.[67]

During the summer of 1998, Tisdale and his supporters received still more threatening calls and letters. One to Tisdale was from Boston and read, "You are a dead man walking".

On the night of July 21, 1998, an explosion rocked the Tisdale home. Someone had blown up the house next door. Jackson Police Sergeant Jim French allowed at the time, "It's suspicious that it occurred next to Mr. Tisdale's home.... Over the years the *Advocate* has angered local politicians, hate groups – they print exactly what they feel they need to print. That tends to anger some people".[68]

Later in 1998 several Jackson City Council members became the subjects of two separate federal investigations. Council President Louis Armstrong and his son Artie pled guilty to receiving a bribe from a strip-club owner in return for a favorable decision on zoning.

In May of 2000 the *Advocate* offices were broken into and bank documents and records were removed. Jackson City Councilman Kenneth Stokes said, "If they even broke a window in [mainstream newspaper] The Clarion-Ledger, it would be everybody and their brother in law-enforcement out there trying to find out who did it".[69]

In May of 2003 as Tisdale was doing a live radio program, a caller promised that he would be shot as he left the station.

* * *

The United Nations Declaration on Human Rights Defenders states in Article 6 "everyone has the right, individually and in association with

---

[67] *News Media Update*, 15 June 1998.

[68] Anne Rochell, 'Newspaper Publisher Haunted by Fiery Attacks', *Atlanta Journal-Constitution*, 20 August 1998.

[69] Ibid.

others... freely to publish, impart or disseminate to others views, information and knowledge on all human rights and fundamental freedoms".

Article 11 of the Declaration states "everyone has the right, individually and in association with others, to the lawful exercise of his or her occupation or profession". Article 12 states that

> The State shall take all necessary measures to ensure the protection by the competent authorities of everyone, individually and in association with others, against any violence, threats, retaliation, *de facto* or *de jure* adverse discrimination, pressure or any other arbitrary action as a consequence of his or her legitimate exercise of the rights referred to in the present Declaration.

At the age of 77, Charles Tisdale is in his office regularly, editing news stories, writing a weekly column, and, as he says, trying to make sure that the *Advocate* "survives my mortality".

Tisdale continues to receive death threats on a regular basis. Law enforcement authorities operate under the assumption that threats come from members of the Ku Klux Klan, but Tisdale sees something more complex and more sinister. He believes that the intimidation, harassment, and threats originate with members of the Central City Investors group, who hire Klansmen to carry them out. Tisdale is convinced that the CCI has decided to put him out of business and to gain control of the newspaper business in Jackson.

Tisdale remains concerned for the solvency of his newspaper. He continues to have difficulty securing advertising from white-owned businesses. And in 2003 alone, $5 million in city funding went to competing newspapers. During recent elections in Mississippi, the *Advocate* received no advertising from candidates, and no white candidate agreed to an editorial board meeting at the paper.

The experience of Charles Tisdale and the *Jackson Advocate* is of course important in its own right – for the many people harmed, for the city of Jackson, and for the ultimate triumph of will and spirit. But it becomes even more significant when one considers how emblematic that experience is of the experience of so many African American human rights and civil rights advocates and activists. Early in his tenure there were the straightforward attacks of racists. Later this became more complex as greed – black and white – preyed upon racial divisions to control economic resources. Tisdale and his staff experienced the collusion of national, state and local law enforcement in illegal surveillance of suspected political opponents. Their mission – to bring the power of information to disenfranchised Blacks – was perceived as a clear and immediate danger by vested interests both Black and white.

Tisdale promises, "I'm not going to be intimidated. I am not afraid.... the *Advocate* has never missed an edition; it will always be here".

US Army Captain James Yee
Fort Benning, Georgia

*"The military's mean-spirited and incompetent prosecution of Captain
James Yee, the former Muslim chaplain at Guantanamo Bay, illustrates the
danger of allowing the war on terrorism to trump basic rights"*
– New York Times Editorial, December 14, 2003

On September 11, 2003, US Army Chaplain James Yee was due to fly home
from his assignment at the US military base at Guantanamo Bay, Cuba, for a
one-week leave at his home in Olympia, Washington. His wife Huda was
waiting for him at the Seattle-Tacoma airport with their four-year old
daughter Sarah.

He never arrived.

A few days later the Federal Bureau of Investigation (FBI) searched the Yee
home, but would tell Huda nothing. Not until ten days later did she learn
from television news that her husband had been arrested and was being held
in a military prison on suspicion of espionage. Huda Yee says, "I saw all the
news, all the bad news about my husband. I didn't believe it. I fell down. I
got sick". James and Huda Yee had been plunged into a long, strange ordeal
of imprisonment, solitary confinement, humiliation, and disgrace.

Chaplain Yee had been taken into custody on September 10, by the FBI at
the Naval Air Station in Jacksonville, Florida, a stopover on his flight home.
Customs agents, tipped off by officials at Guantanamo, claimed to have
found "suspicious papers" in Yee's backpack: four notebooks and notepads,
other "printed papers", and a list of names of detainees. But Yee's attorneys
said that the papers consisted largely of web pages on Middle East history.

Front Line is concerned that Chaplain Yee was arbitrarily detained and the
victim of a politically motivated prosecution because of his work to defend
the human rights of Guantanamo detainees, including freedom of religion.

* * *

Camp Delta is the maximum-security facility at Guantanamo, composed of
concrete block cells, interrogation trailers, guard towers, and rings of razor

wire. Two-thousand US troops and civilian personnel provide for the imprisonment of 660 detainees from over forty countries. Most were captured in Afghanistan during US combat with the Taliban and brought to Guantanamo during January and February of 2002 and are considered terrorist suspects by the USA. Nearly all are Muslim.

Although held for more than two years, the detainees have not been afforded hearings to determine whether they participated in any conflict or committed any crime. The Uniform Code of Military Conduct is the essential guide for American courts-martial and other proceedings of military law. The Code provides military convicts the right to appeal to civilian judges. Guantanamo prisoners, when they are tried by military commissions, will not have that right.

The US Government maintains that because the detainees were taken into custody on "foreign land", they may be held indefinitely without charge or trial. Yet they have not been accorded the status of prisoners of war. The US also claims that because the prisoners are held on land that is not US sovereign territory, they do not have the right to recourse in US courts. In fact, the Government has "complete jurisdiction and control" over Guantanamo by virtue of a perpetual lease agreement made with Cuba in 1903.

Human Rights Watch reported in January 2004 that,

> None of those detainees has received any sort of hearing or judicial review. Scores of Guantanamo detainees were farmers, taxi drivers and laborers with no ties to al-Quaeda or the Taliban.... In humanitarian terms, prolonged and indefinite detention can have a devastating psychological impact on detainees. Indeed, thirty-four suicide attempts have been recorded at Guantanamo to date. One of the former detainees interviewed by Human Rights Watch confirmed that he had attempted suicide three times at Guantanamo....Two years on, the rules of law continue to buckle under the weight of the US detention camp at Guantanamo Bay.[70]

---

[70] *United States: Guantanamo Two Years On*, Human Rights Watch, 9 January 2004.

Five-hundred and fifty of the 660 are held in maximum security. In return for their cooperation, they are brought out of their cells in leg-irons and handcuffs for one-half hour of exercise, a shower, and a change of clothes five times a week; prisoners who are less cooperative are allowed out only twice a week. A Guantanamo cell is a fifty-four-sqare foot metal box a bit larger than a large mattress. There is no air conditioning; guards turn on ceiling fans in hallways when the temperature rises above eighty-six degrees Fahrenheit. Lights stay on throughout the night.[71]

Amnesty International has found,

> Camp X-Ray and its successor Camp Delta, have become synonymous with a government's pursuit of unfettered executive power and disregard for the rule of law. The jailing of hundreds of men at Guantanamo Bay without charge or trial— some for two years—is an affront to justice, violates human dignity, and is a shameful stain on the US record.[72]

The Red Cross conducted a two-month investigation at Guantanamo. According to an article by Marjorie Cohn, its report said that investigators had

> Observed a worrying decline in the psychological health of a large number of [the detainees].... The US authorities have placed the internees in Guantanamo beyond the law. This means that, after more than eighteen months of captivity, the internees still have no idea about their fate, and no means of recourse through any legal mechanism.[73]

In "The Dark Art of Interrogation", an article in the Atlantic Monthly, journalist Mark Bowden detailed the interrogation of Khalid Sheik Mohammed:

> He would most likely have been locked naked in a cell with no trace of daylight. The space would be filled night and day with

---

[71] *Vanity Fair*, January 2004, 90.

[72] *Holding Human Rights Hostage*, Amnesty International USA, 24 December 2003.

[73] Marjorie Cohn, 'Wrong Treatment in the Wrong Place', *Counterpunch*, 17 January 2004.

harsh light and noise, and would be so small that he would be
unable to stand upright, to sit comfortably, or to recline fully.
He would be kept awake, cold, and probably wet. If he
managed to doze, he would be roughly awakened. He would be
fed infrequently and irregularly, and then only with thin,
tasteless meals. Isolated, confused, weary, hungry, frightened,
and tormented, Sheik Mohammed would gradually be reduced
to a seething collection of simple needs, all of them controlled
by his interrogators.[74]

In January, 2002, Secretary of Defense Donald Rumsfeld was asked why the
Geneva Convention did not apply to the detainees. He replied that he did not
have "the slightest concern" for their treatment after what they had done.[75]

* * *

James Yee, 35, was born in Naperville, Illinois, and raised as a Lutheran in
Springfield, New Jersey, twenty miles west of Manhattan. He is Chinese-
American and a Muslim convert.

In 1990, Yee graduated from the US Army's elite academy, West Point, then
served active duty as an air artillery officer. He left the Army in 1996 and
moved to Syria to study Islam. When he returned two years later, he re-
entered the Army as an Islamic chaplain.

Yee's father Joseph served two years in the US Army during World War
Two. In addition to James, his second and third sons also served. Following
his son's arrest, Joseph Yee was not allowed to have contact with him for
three weeks. Media trucks parked in front of his home, and reporters phoned
constantly. He stopped answering the phone and put a sign on his door
discouraging reporters.

Joseph Lee says, "After 9/11, my son did a lot of PR work for the Army
about keeping Muslims in the Army and the military, and to calm down
some of those fears. This was done to improve their image".

---

[74] Mark Bowden, 'The Dark Art of Interrogation', *Atlantic Monthly*, October 2003.
[75] *The Economist*, January 2002.

141

Chaplin Yee himself has said, "When I go into the field, I have a copy of the Koran and next to it a copy of the US Constitution". After the September 11 attacks, Yee stated, "An attack of terrorism, the taking of innocent civilian lives, is prohibited by Islam, and whoever has done these deeds needs to be brought to justice, whether he is Muslim or not". He made a concerted effort to speak in churches and mosques, schools and colleges, to explain that Islam is not a violent religion. Acquaintances of Yee in his hometown of Olympia, Washington, say he spoke with passion of his loyalty to the US and to the military.

Yee began his duties at Guantanamo in November 2002, when he was assigned to minister to the spiritual needs of the large majority of Muslim detainees. He interviewed them about their needs, guided their studies, and led them in prayer.

Yee arranged broadcasts of recorded calls to Muslim prayers five times a day; when his CD player broke he chanted prayers into a microphone. He provided prisoners with assurances that food was being prepared according to Islamic dietary codes, and arranged for a change in meal times so detainees could observe daytime fasting during Ramadan. He made sure that every person had a copy of the Koran and a place to keep it so it would not touch the ground.[76]

He briefed his army superiors on many issues related to Islam, including the history of the religion, and possible reasons for the rise in suicide attempts at the camp. He helped resolve misunderstandings and conflicts between prisoners and prison authorities.

During his ten months at Guantanamo, the army put Yee forward to the media as a "model Muslim in uniform" and often chose him to speak with journalists. The Pentagon used his presence to demonstrate that it was providing humanitarian services. He received several medals and commendations; one read, "Yee's strong sense of professionalism, maturity and dedication to duty reflect credit upon himself, the US Army and the Department of Defense".

Sarah Kershaw, 'Army Chaplain in Detention Sought to Teach About Islam', *New York Times*, 24 September 2003.

Following the removal of Captain Yee from his duties at Guantanamo, no Muslim cleric has been assigned to serve the religious needs of the detainees, and the Pentagon has no plans to appoint one, stating, "There was never an intent to provide a designated spiritual leader to the detainees".[77] Yee's responsibilities were assumed by the head chaplain, Colonel Steve Feehan, who, as he says, comes "from the conservative strand of the Southern Baptist Church". Feehan's faith teaches him that, "Without believing in and accepting Christ, without faith, you cannot be redeemed. It's impossible".[78]

* * *

The accusations against Yee first surfaced in the Washington [DC] Times on September 20, 2003. The Times is owned by Rev. Sun Yung Moon, and has close ties to the most conservative elements of the Bush Administration.

The Times reported that five charges were being considered against Yee: sedition; aiding the enemy; spying; espionage; and failure to obey a general order. According to reporter Rowan Scarborough, the order to arrest Yee came from "the highest levels" of government.[79]

Various "authorities", speaking always on condition of anonymity, repeatedly used terms such as "sedition" and "espionage". Typical of the media coverage was this: "A Defense official, speaking on condition of anonymity, described the charges as 'preliminary', necessary to keep holding Captain Yee, but said that the Army continues to investigate him and additional charges may be filed".[80]

A leak from the FBI claimed that Yee was caught with "classified documents that may have included sketches or diagrams of Guantanamo's high security prison, Camp Delta, along with lists of detainees and their interrogators".[81] And the New York Times reported, "Investigators are looking into the possibility that [Yee] was sympathetic to prisoners and he was preparing to aid them in some undetermined way".[82]

---

[77] Pentagon press release, 6 January 2004.

[78] *Vanity Fair.*

[79] Rowan Scarbourough, *Washington Times*, 20 September 2003.

[80] Will Durham, 'US Army Chaplain Yee Charges in Guantanamo Case', *Muslim News*, 10 October 2003.

[81] Cheryl Fiandoca, WABC Radio News, 20 September 2003.

[82] *New York Times*, 21 September 2003.

Partly because of the official silence on Yee's case, speculation became rife. Several publications suggested that Yee was planning to expose the brutal treatment of some of the detainees.

Later in September, high-ranking officers at Guantanamo, told a military judge that Yee would be charged with espionage, sedition, mutiny, and aiding the enemy, crimes that are punishable by death. But according to a senior official at the Department of Justice, the FBI and other civilian law enforcement officials did not believe that the evidence against Yee warranted prosecution.

The military's pursuit of Yee may have originated with inexperienced intelligence officials at Guantanamo who felt pressure to find some form of infiltration. One of these counterintelligence officers was himself charged with wrongfully transporting classified documents, but was not detained or pursued. In addition, senior officials at Guantanamo were suspicious and resentful of Muslims being involved with the lives of the detainees. Officials initially seemed to think that Yee might be part of a large-scale terrorist plot to infiltrate Guantanamo.

Reacting to reports of the charges, Ibrahim Hooper, director of The Council on American-Islamic Relations, said,

> I think the Muslim community and Arab-American community are shell-shocked at this point. They're seeing a stream, a drumbeat of these kinds of incidents, one after the other. And we're not seeing support from political circles, from elected officials, from opinion leaders. In fact, why aren't we hearing President Bush come out and defend the patriotism of thousands of American Muslims who are serving loyally in the military?[83]

On October 10, 2003, a full month after being arrested, Captain Yee was charged with two counts of violating Article 92 of the Uniform Code of Military Justice: "failing to obey a general order" by "wrongfully taking classified material to a housing unit", and "wrongfully transporting

---

[83] Interview with Wolf Blitzer, CNN, 26 September 2003.

classified material without proper security containers or covers". But there was no mention of the more serious charges of espionage and sedition.

Yee was held in maximum security at the Naval Consolidated Brig in Charleston, South Carolina, for nearly three months along with suspected terrorists designated as highly dangerous. For much of that time he was kept in solitary confinement.[84]

After one month of being held incommunicado, he was allowed two fifteen-minute telephone calls per day, but was prevented from communicating with his wife. Eugene Fidell, Yee's civilian attorney, said that for the first six weeks Yee was "kept in isolation in a small cell for twenty-three hours a day. He was required to wear irons when leaving his cell". Guards refused to tell Yee the time of day, or the direction to face to help him pray toward Mecca. Fidell believes that Yee was treated considerably worse that the Guantanamo prisoners.[85]

Yee was released on November 23, one day after his attorney wrote to President Bush saying that Yee's treatment and punishment were excessive. His letter pointed out that, "If everyone who failed to safeguard classified information according to the letter of the law was arrested, the brigs would be full to capacity and then some". He noted that the former director of the Central Intelligence Agency John Deutsch had received only a reprimand for the same offense. He went on to say, "Yee is being treated as if he were an enemy combatant rather than a commissioned officer".[86]

* * *

On November 24, US Southern Command announced an investigation into new alleged violations of the Uniform Code of Military Justice, saying that they would "explore the possibility" that Yee had an extramarital affair, and had pornographic material stored on his computer. He was also charged with "misleading a superior officer", supposedly by saying that several compact discs had been designated appropriate for detainees.[87]

---

[84] Neil Lewis, *New York Times*, 26 November 2003.

[85] Sarah Kershaw, 'Guantanamo Chaplain and His Wife Speak Out', *New York Times*, 5 December 2003.

[86] Frank Davies and Carol Rosenberg, "Muslim Army Chaplain Released, Faces New Charges", Knight Ridder Newspapers, 25 November 2003.

[87] Lewis.

Once Yee was released, the Government began to distance itself from the allegations of espionage. None of the new charges — allegations that he cheated on his wife, stored pornography on a government-issued laptop computer, lied to military personnel — had any relation to spying. Yet each charge was punishable under the Uniform Code of Military Justice. If convicted at a court martial on all counts, Yee could have been sentenced to thirteen years in a military prison. Conviction on each of these new charges would have carried the potential for two years in prison, dishonorable discharge, and forfeiture of pay. Attorney Fidell said, "I would hope that the military justice system would have a lot better use for its resources than to prosecute chaplains for adultery".

Under military law, a soldier must be brought to trial within 120 days of his arrest. Yee was arrested ninety days before the aborted hearing, but 130 days before the new hearing date of January 19, which also resulted in a postponement.

Fidell argued that the military was pursuing the new charges to cover up its mistake in suggesting Yee was guilty of treason.

> We're thrilled that Chaplain Yee was released, but on the other hand, the additional charges are the kind of thing that gives military justice a bad name…. They have destroyed this man's reputation for what turns out to be no good reason, and now it appears they are pursuing matters in a completely vindictive manner.

For Huda Yee, a Muslim, the allegations of adultery were more hurtful than the suspicion of espionage: "All my family is shocked. My mother cried, and she is still crying", and "It is clear the government is only trying to destroy his character and his family. They will not succeed". Friend and neighbor Shaheed Nuriddin says, "The adultery was worse. The Army came to her and said, 'You didn't know the man you married'. And this was after they kept trying to get her to identify her husband as a terrorist".

Upon his release, Yee was transferred to Fort Benning in Georgia, restricted to administrative tasks, and barred from contact with anyone associated with

Guantanamo. Huda, Sarah and Yee's parents have moved to a hotel near the base.

Leaders of the American Muslim community charged that US politicians tried to exploit the arrest of Yee to marginalize American Muslims. Ibrahim Hooper of the Council on American-Islamic Relations said,

> He was defamed and smeared and accused of being a spy. Then all of a sudden, they're not even sorry. They're saying, 'You can go now, and for good measure we'll throw in a few charges to further damage your reputation'. It's a very suspicious scenario that developed.

Ted Wang, the policy director of Chinese for Affirmative Action, said,

> That the military went to such lengths to leak the information and pursue aggressive disciplinary actions causes some concern that it was motivated because of his religion, the kinds of services he provided to prisoners, or possibly his race.[88]

Cecilia Chang, president of Justice for New Americans, said, "The Government had nothing on him, especially not espionage. The new charges are minor ones that are normally handled administratively and never warrant maximum confinement". Philip Ting, executive director of Asia Law Center, is concerned that leaks from "unnamed military sources" prejudiced investigators and the public against Yee. "Outlets like the New York Times ran front-page coverage of the story and several follow-ups. News of the release appeared on page 22".

* * *

On December 9, 2003, at Fort Benning, the criminal hearing against Yee became confused when military prosecutors requested more time to ascertain if the papers found in Yee's possession were, in fact, classified documents. Prosecutors had given reams of papers to defense lawyers, but then asked for their return because the documents had mistakenly been designated as classified.

---

[88] WBAI Radio, 11 November, 2003.

Defense attorneys had repeatedly lodged complaints that they could not proceed while it remained unclear whether the documents in Yee's possession were classified or not. The Government capitulated and sought a delay to review the documents. The hearing was postponed until January 19, 2004.[89]

Army officials declined comment on whether any document had been marked with a classification. United States Southern Command spokesman Lt. Colonel Bill Costello said, "I can't comment on what should've happened or did happen or hasn't happened".[90]

The Army also sought suspension of the hearing because they had learned that military prosecutors had mistakenly mishandled classified documents by sending analyzed pages of Yee's diary to investigators. Said Fidell, "What they did is very, very similar to what they claim my client did. And they're supposed to know best of all". Fidell called it "disgraceful" that Yee should have been imprisoned for seventy-six days for having documents that the Government still has not determined were sensitive.[91]

Also on December 9, one of Yee's lawyers, former prosecutor Major Scott Sykes, said that military prosecutors told him that they might seek the death penalty for Yee.[92]

As the Government's case against Yee appeared to be falling apart, reaction set in among the nation's journalists. One newspaper reporter in Atlanta asked a Pentagon official,

> Does the Defense Department plan to arrest all the *other* adulterers it learns about? Will the US soon be using its amazing new arrest-anybody powers to imprison Internet-

---

[89] Neil Lewis, 'Prosecutors Say It's Unclear Papers Chaplain Carried Were Classified', *New York Times*, 10 December 2003.

[90] Carol Rosenberg, 'Classified Data Confusion Delays Chaplain's Hearing', *Miami Herald*, 10 December 2003.

[91] Ibid.

[92] Lewis, 10th December 2003

148

browsing soldiers in Iraq, adulterous Congressmen, and at least
one former Director of Central Intelligence?[93]

The Washington Times reported, "The Army has suspended a pretrial
hearing for Captain James Yee, a Muslim chaplain, while the military does
something it should have done before the proceeding—screen the evidence
for classified material". The Times also reported that the customs agent who
stopped Yee had been tipped to detain him. A government source told the
Times that Yee had been under surveillance while he was at Guantanamo.[94]

On December 14, 2003, the New York Times weighed in with this opinion:

> The military's mean-spirited and incompetent prosecution of
> Captain James Yee, the former Muslim chaplain at Guantanamo
> Bay, illustrates the danger of allowing the war on terrorism to
> trump basic rights.... In the interests of justice, and of
> resurrecting their own reputation, military prosecutors should
> drop the case.... Rather than put the questions about the charges
> to rest right away, the military led off its case against Captain
> Yee last week with evidence he had an affair with a female
> officer, testimony that his wife and child had to listen to as they
> sat in court. It has also accused him of keeping pornography on
> a government computer. These charges in no way suggest that
> he was a security threat, and they are the kind the military
> generally does not bother to bring. They seem to be motivated,
> in this case, by a desire to embarrass Captain Yee, and by
> frustration that the larger case against him is so weak.... It is
> already clear how much harm the military's misguided
> prosecution has done to Captain Yee and his family. What is
> less obvious, but no less real, is the threat this sort of
> prosecutorial mentality poses to all Americans. The specter of
> terrorism cannot become an excuse for the Government to
> railroad people first, and ask questions later.[95]

The British newspaper, The Independent, put it this way:

[93] Colin Campbell, *Atlanta Journal-Constitution*, 11 December 2003.
[94] Rowan Scarborough, 'Yee Case on Hold As Military Falters', *Washington Times*, 12 December 2003.
[95] Editorial, 'Captain Yee's Ordeal', *New York Times*, 14 December 2003.

The status [enemy combatants] does not exist under international law, or that of the United States, which explains the Pentagon's insistence that the detainees are not subject to the jurisdiction of any state, including that of the United States. Such niceties as innocence until proof of guilt, the right to know the charges against one, the right to a prompt trial, and the rules of gathering evidence are, therefore, irrelevant. Not only that, but the status is effectively permanent. It lasts for the duration of the war on terror.[96]

Major General John Fugh, once the highest-ranking uniformed legal officer in the Army said,

This whole thing makes the military prosecutors look ridiculous. It certainly seems like they couldn't get him on what they first thought they had, so they said, 'Let's get the son of a gun on something'. Adding these Mickey Mouse charges just makes them look dumb.[97]

In February, the Army delayed Yee's hearing for the fifth time, rescheduling it for March 10, 2004, but it was delayed yet again.

On April 14, 2004, the remaining allegations against Yee — adultery and downloading pornography — were rejected. General Hill of US Southern Command ruled that the reprimand punishment would be lifted and would not be entered on Yee's military record. Captain Yee therefore stands cleared of all charges.

* * *

On April 20, 2004, the United States Supreme Court heard arguments on the issue of whether the detainees at Guantanamo were entitled to any judicial oversight of the legality of their detentions by means of *habeas corpus* relief. The Court will make a decision by early July on this crucial issue. During the arguments several Justices expressed unease with the Administration's

---

[96] *The Independent*, 13 January 2004.

[97] Neil Lewis and Thom Shanker, 'Missteps Seen in Muslim Chaplain's Spy Case', *New York Times*, 4 January 2004.

arguments that there was no room for judicial oversight of these detentions because they were wartime detainees.

Front Line, along with many international human rights organizations, contends that there is no such thing as a "human rights free" zone and that the detainees are entitled to the full protection of their rights under international humanitarian and human rights law. Hopefully, the US Supreme Court will reach this conclusion under US law but the United States is bound by established international law to provide such protections to the Guantanamo detainees.

* * *

The United Nations Declaration on Human Rights Defenders states in Article 8 that everyone has

> The right, individually and in association with others, to submit to governmental bodies and agencies and organizations concerned with public affairs criticism and proposals for improving their functioning and to draw attention to any aspect of their work that may hinder or impede the promotion, protection and realization of human rights and fundamental freedoms.

Article 11 of the Declaration states that "everyone has the right, individually and in association with others, to the lawful exercise of his or her occupation or profession." Article 12 states that

> Everyone is entitled, individually and in association with others, to be protected effectively under national law in reacting against or opposing, through peaceful means, activities and acts, including those by omission, attributable to States that result in violations of human rights and fundamental freedoms, as well as acts of violence perpetrated by groups or individuals that affect the enjoyment of human rights and fundamental freedoms.

Analysis, Conclusions and Recommendations

The cases presented in this report raise serious concerns regarding the protection of human rights defenders in the United States and about the respect for international human rights within the United States. For the most part human rights defenders in the United States are able to operate freely and safely. In many other parts of the world, human rights defenders and advocates suffer more severe violations with greater frequency. Constant repression, arbitrary arrest, systematic torture, disappearances and political killings are common features in the lives of human rights activists in many countries. This is not the situation in the United States. The United States has in place a broad variety of protections for the activities of human rights defenders, from the protections offered by the Constitution to local ordinances.

However, the cases featured in this report illustrate how human rights defenders in the US can be denied employment, threatened, harassed, beaten, arrested, abused, unjustifiably prosecuted and be traced unfairly in the criminal justice system because of their work. Those who receive the worst treatment are often those most active in protecting and promoting the rights of the most vulnerable in US society or those who are perceived to be challenging the prerogatives of the powerful. Such treatment appears to be most often accorded those defending the rights of minorities or challenging the fundamental distribution of economic and social power in American society.

Since September 11th there have been new challenges to human rights defenders arising out of the "war on terrorism". This report touches on these challenges through the experiences of three defenders, but the challenge posed by this "war" to the entire international human rights framework is profound and ongoing. These new challenges underscore the urgent need for international solidarity between human rights defenders throughout the world because the "war on terrorism" is global and potentially unending.

A. Human Rights Defenders and Human Rights Abuses in the United States

1. Human Rights Defenders and the "War on Terrorism"

"They that can give up essential liberty to obtain a little temporary safety deserve neither"—Benjamin Franklin, 1759.

"Witness five faces of a human rights policy fixated on freedom from fear. First, closed government and invasions of privacy. Second, scapegoating immigrants and refugees. Third, creating extra-legal zones, most prominently at the naval base at Guantanamo Bay in Cuba. Fourth, creating extra-legal persons, particularly the detainees of American citizenship labeled 'enemy combatants.' Fifth, a reduced American human rights presence throughout the rest of the world."
- *Harold Hongju Koh, former US Assistant Secretary of State for Democracy, Human Rights and Labor*

Since the terrorist attacks of September 11, 2001, the US Administration has expanded its capacity and its willingness to invade private personal lives in the name of national security. Previously restricted from gathering domestic political intelligence, the Federal Bureau of Investigation (FBI), has been given new latitude to monitor the activities of individuals and organizations within the USA, including the activities of human rights defenders. The Government has developed programs for drawing individual characteristics from the enormous quantity of personal data acquired by local, state and federal agencies, by banks and businesses, by periodicals and associations. Law enforcement agencies throughout the country have been given a broader mandate to participate in aggressive efforts to root out potential terrorists. The exercise of these new powers has led to widespread alarm about the infringement of civil liberties in the United States and concern that the abuses of prior eras will occur again.

As the cases of human rights defenders Lynne Stewart, James Yee, and Farouk Abdel-Muhti demonstrate, the "war on terrorism" has led to the surveillance, arrest, incarceration and prosecution of human rights defenders in circumstances indicating that their human rights activities are the reason for these actions.

Of the twelve defenders in this report, seven have been the subjects of domestic intelligence operations by US law enforcement agencies. Such activities in the modern era began with the anti-communist witch hunts of the early 1950s. FBI Director J. Edgar Hoover extended his investigatory powers to monitor and discredit advocates he deemed threats to the USA, for any reasons. His "suspects" included civil rights activists like Martin Luther King, Robert F. Kennedy, and Cesar Chavez. In the late 1960s and early 1970s, the FBI mounted its Cointelpro operation to manufacture or suppress evidence, impugn personal integrity, suborn witnesses, and harass activists.

As a direct result of these excesses, Congress imposed tight restrictions on the ability of national agencies to undertake domestic political investigations. Other limitations are established as a result of litigation in the 1980s. These limitations were relaxed during the Reagan Administration. With the adoption of the PATRIOT Act on October 24, 2001, the creation of the Department of Homeland Security, and the direction of the Department of Justice (DOJ) under Attorney General John Ashcroft, restraints on domestic intelligence gathering have been increasingly abandoned. Given the history of the Cointelpro abuses, human rights defenders in the United States are concerned that their lawful activities may be surveyed or disrupted without adequate oversight or safeguards.

The Department of Justice has charged Lynne Stewart with, among other things, "providing material support to a foreign terrorist organization". This crime was introduced in the Anti-Terrorism and Effective Death Penalty Act of 1996 (AEDPA). In 2000 the US Ninth Circuit Court of Appeals ruled that definitions and assumed meanings of "material support" were unconstitutionally vague. But the PATRIOT Act extended the definition still further, and prosecutors are now using the statute more and more often. David Cole, professor of international law at Georgetown University, has said that the law "would make it a crime for a Quaker to send a book on Gandhi's theory of nonviolence to the leader of a terrorist group". This breadth of the statute also enables selective persecution based on the political or religious beliefs of the targets of government investigations.

The PATRIOT Act has made it easier for government agencies to gather data and assemble profiles on US residents. Sections 215 and 505 of the act permit the FBI to gather data covertly — from financial, medical, library and internet records — on US residents without having to demonstrate any basis for suspicion of terrorism or other criminal acts. Approvals for such investigations are considered in secret proceedings of the Foreign Intelligence Surveillance Court (FISC). Section 505 provides that "National Security Letters" may allow the FBI access to telephone and internet records without judicial oversight of any kind. Federal agents may use intrusive surveillance techniques such as wiretaps simply by indicating that they are to be used in connection with foreign intelligence.

On January 28, 2003, the White House announced the creation of the Terrorist Threat Integration Center (TTIC), which functions as a law enforcement central command on terrorism. It can call on the FBI, the CIA, the National Security Agency, the Department of Homeland Security, the Department of Justice, the Department of Defense, and the Department of State. The TTIC can dispatch agents and capacities of these agencies and others to gather information; such data would be shared by all. The Joint Terrorism Task Force (JTTF) has permitted anti-terror programs and the Department of Homeland Security to make law enforcement administrators and officers throughout the United States—national, regional, state and local—partners in surveillance, monitoring, and reporting of "suspicious" behavior. By virtue of Executive Order (E.O. 13292), the Government has new latitude to restrict information from the public and to alter the classification of documents to higher levels of secrecy. These measures raise serious constitutional and international human rights issues, especially concerning the rights to privacy.

The desire to improve intelligence capacities in the wake of 9/11 is entirely understandable, but removing judicial oversight and hard fought restraints on intelligence gathering increases the likelihood of abuses. The absence of debate about the necessity for safeguards and the apparent quest for security at the expense of civil liberties interests has created a climate of unease and fear for human rights defenders who advocate for the rights of groups, including religious groups, who have become targets of the "war on terrorism".

The selective detention of thousands of non-citizens since September 11th, including Farouk Abdel-Muhti, usually on technical immigration charges, has not resulted in any "terrorism" prosecutions and has disrupted the lives and well being of thousands of immigrant families without any gain in national security.

It is difficult to escape the conclusion that the "war on terrorism" has been waged in an indiscriminate manner that threatens human rights and human rights defenders in the United States, as well as the other places in the world where this "war" is fought. Those at greatest risk are the very people whose rights are defended by some of the advocates featured in this report: immigrants, Arab-Americans and Muslims. But also at high risk are opponents of the war in Iraq, anti-militarization and peace activists, advocates for civil rights and liberties, proponents of economic and social justice, and people who simply choose to live unconventional lives.

2. Detention and Imprisonment of Human Rights Defenders

"Over two million people are held in jails and prisons in the United States, the highest proportion relative to population of any country in the world. The vast majority are poor. Over half are African American; one of every fourteen African American males is incarcerated. Although comprising only twenty-four percent of the total population, African American and Hispanic prisoners comprise sixty-three percent of the prison population. One and a half million children in the United States have a parent in prison"
— *US Human Rights Network*[98]

Human rights defenders in the United States generally have excellent access to information, representation and support. They are not usually imprisoned solely for their advocacy, and even when they are it is not for a long period of time. But defenders such as Cheri Honkala, Jeff Dietrich, Lynne Stewart and Chokwe Lumumba do attract police attention and surveillance as a result of their activities. As the cases of Honkala and Dietrich make clear, repeated acts of civil disobedience will result in increasingly frequent and severe detention. The cases of Jeff Dietrich, James Yee and Farouk Abdel-Muhti raise serious concerns that the severity of their incarceration may be attributable to their activities and beliefs.

In the United States, imprisonment means that you are likely to be the victim of violent assault or sexual abuse. You are likely to experience discriminatory and arbitrary discipline. You are likely to be exposed to

---

[98] US Human Rights Network (2002), *Something Inside So Strong*, Washington DC: US Human Rights Network, at p. 18.

disease, especially HIV/AIDS, hepatitis and tuberculosis; if you receive health care it will be inadequate.[99] This state of affairs exists because there is little public support for the idea that prisoners are entitled to basic human rights.

This forfeit of rights extends beyond the prison sentence. Most of the thirteen million people who have been convicted of a felony in the USA (almost seven percent of the adult population) permanently lose the right to vote, to receive student loans or public housing, and to claim many parental rights.[100]

Eleven of the defenders in this report have had occasion to advocate for people in prison; seven have been detained or imprisoned as a direct result of their activism; seven are either on probation or have charges pending. Farouk Abdel-Muhti was imprisoned without criminal charge for over two years.

It also appears that prison officials use solitary confinement and sensory deprivation far more often than is generally recognized. Even minor infractions of prison rules can cause a detainee to be held in solitary confinement for long periods of time. This appears to be even more likely if the prisoner has been charged with an offense that has political content. James Yee, Jeff Dietrich and Farouk Abdel-Muhti all experienced punishment by isolation, Yee even before he was charged.

The USA increasingly turns to incarceration to attack the symptoms of fundamental social failings it does not have the will to address: racial bias, poverty, drug use, mental illness. And as the work of Abdel-Muhti and Enrique Morones demonstrates, incarceration is being used more and more frequently to address concerns about immigration and "terrorism".

3. Racism and Human Rights Defenders

Racial prejudice continues to be a major problem in the USA. Formal segregation and Jim Crow laws may be gone, but racism and discrimination –both subtle and blatant – still exist.

---

[99] US Human Rights Network (2002).

[100] Jennifer Fonnerman, *Life on the Outside: The Prison Odyssey of Elaine Bartlet*, quoted in *New York Times*, 21 March 2004, Sunday Book Review, p. 7.

Charles Tisdale must still protect himself and his newspaper from attacks by the Ku Klux Klan and other racists. If the Danns were white Americans, it is unlikely they would be enduring armed intrusions and seizures of their property. As a Chinese American Muslim, James Yee offers a doubly attractive target for military investigation. The treatment suffered by Enrique Morones appears to be a direct consequence of his Latino heritage. The treatment Farouk Abdel-Muhti has received exemplifies American prejudice toward Arabs and Muslims, which has only grown over the last three years. The brutalization and enslavement fought by the Immokalee Workers is suffered almost solely by Hispanic victims. And Chokwe Lumumba has spoken of the disparagement and disrespect shown by white Americans toward things that matter most to African Americans—their leaders, their art and music, and for some, Islam.

In the course of gathering information for this report, a disproportionate number of complaints came from one state: Mississippi. This reflects Mississippi's history of racism and human rights violations and suggests how difficult it is to remedy such long standing violations. This is also a reflection of the vibrancy of the human rights advocacy in Mississippi. It is the reason this report concerns so many defenders from one state.

4. Human Rights Defenders and Privatization

This report shows a clear trend toward the privatization of public space and services. From the downtown districts of Jeff Dietrich's Los Angeles and Charles Tisdale's Jackson to the open range land of Carrie and Mary Dann's Western Shoshone nation, there is pressure to restrict free access, to turn previously open public spaces to closed private areas, and to deploy private security forces to uphold the restrictions. Human rights defenders who challenge this phenomenon pay the consequences.

These limits on access and the emphasis on protection of private property partially explains the frequent aggressive overreaction of police. Cheri Honkala, Jeff Dietrich, Chokwe Lumumba and the Charleston Five have all been victims of violent police tactics responding to peaceful protest. The sanctity of private property and Government complicity in its encroachment on public land explains in part the enforcement overkill confronting Carrie and Mary Dann.

158

Increasingly, human rights defenders are confronting violations by private security and paramilitary personnel. Brenda and Wanda Henson have endured the excesses of a private militia insufficiently restrained by local officials. Charles Tisdale confronts the private law enforcement hired by the developers of Jackson's downtown. Jeff Dietrich protects the homeless against the excesses of private security guards, the "Shirts", in Los Angeles.

Another form of quasi-official action against defenders is the use of basic utility services to harass and punish activism. When the editorial policy of the *Jackson Advocate* under Charles Tisdale became clear, there were disruptions in the office's heat, water, electricity and telephone services. Interruptions in electricity forced the Hensons to delay the opening of their Gulfport bookstore; interruptions continue in the water supply to Camp Sister Spirit. In its lopsided battle with the Danns, the Bureau of Land Management has denied them access to public roads. Officials of the US Department of Housing and Urban Development in Philadelphia would rather have cold and empty buildings than provide shelter for the families defended by Cheri Honkala.

An interesting corollary is illustrated by the cases of Brenda and Wanda Henson, Jeff Dietrich and Chokwe Lumumba. Each of them, and many other advocates, have felt it necessary to establish independent land-based communities of conscience. Apparently unable to find a secure base from which to pursue their advocacy, they have created their own oases for the protection of activists, the training of advocates, and the work of human rights defenders.

5. Human Rights Defenders and Economic, Social and Cultural Rights

"To be a poor man is hard, but to be a poor race in a land of dollars is the very bottom of hardships"- W.E.B. Du Bois, 1903

The United States has a long history of struggle over civil and political rights. There is a network of individuals, organizations, associations, foundations and media outlets that is capable of fighting back when those rights are threatened. The same is not true for economic, social and cultural rights. Mainstream political support for a social welfare state has evaporated. Ken Riley and the Longshoremen notwithstanding, the influence of labor unions has greatly diminished. Universal health care seems more and more remote. Even the minimal "safety net" of welfare, workfare and other social programs has been shredded in recent years.

As a matter of policy, the US Government does not recognize most internationally respected economic and social rights as rights at all. The prevailing US myth continues to be that all Americans have the opportunity to "succeed", to "pull themselves up by their own bootstraps". For many elected officials, the very term "economic rights" still smacks of Communism and is essentially anti-American. According to US Government policy economic and social rights — including the right to adequate food and shelter, quality education and decent employment, and decent health care — are not rights to be respected but privileges to be earned, or to be granted as a matter of policy but not obligation.

In terms of aggregate wealth, the USA is first by far among the nations of the world. Yet, according to the Center for Economic and Social Rights, nearly twenty percent of children under five live in poverty, the highest such rate among industrialized countries.[101] Over 40 million people do not have health insurance. Twenty-eight million must routinely worry about having enough food to eat.

Many of the defenders presented in this report are at the vanguard of a new movement for the protection and promotion of economic and social rights in the USA. Cheri Honkala and Jeff Dietrich provide protections for economically marginalized individuals and families and work for the extension of economic rights for all US residents. Charles Tisdale and the Charleston Five advocate for equal access to decent jobs. Brenda and Wanda Henson and Enrique Morones protect the social and economic rights of individuals falling outside the American norm while advancing the rights of whole segments of the population. Carrie and Mary Dann and the Western Shoshone Defense Project are among a very small corps of advocates for the preservation of traditional cultural rights, especially for indigenous peoples.

This report clearly demonstrates that there is a substantial and growing movement for economic and social justice in the USA. Most of the

---

[101] http://www.cesr.org/PROGRAMS/us%20program/PPEHRCDeclaration.doc

defenders presented in this report have found that, in one way or another, they must address economic discrimination: the systemic protection of those with resources and the grinding down of those without. They must also be concerned about the economic and social threats that they and other defenders face: loss of employment and assets; a record of criminal charges; excessive bail, fines and fees; community ostracism and abuse.

Cheri Honkala defends the economic rights of individuals and families who need her protection precisely because they have been denied resources. Charles Tisdale, after many years of working for civil rights, finds he must focus his efforts on discrimination in economic opportunity. Carrie and Mary Dann, marginally and reluctantly involved in the economy of the dominant society, are deprived of their capacity to make even a meager living. Brenda and Wanda Henson provided for the needs of poor communities both before and after fighting for civil rights. Jeff Dietrich pursues a life of poverty and sacrifice because he believes he must be one with the people he serves. To live in solidarity with their constituents, the Immokalee Workers accept only the wages that a decently paid field worker would earn. As a result of spending "too much" time assisting people without resources, Enrique Morones finds himself without a stable income.

As many of the defender cases demonstrate, the role of the major corporations is a central concern for any movement for economical and social justice in the United States. Despite recent scandals, (e.g. Enron), it is difficult to challenge the entrenched power of major corporations and their adverse impacts on American life. The difficulty of this struggle is illustrated in the cases of Jeff Dietrich, Cheri Honkala, the Charleston Five, the Danns, Enrique Morones and the Immokalee Workers.

In the US, the loss of a job usually means the loss of security. Most Americans have access to quality health care only if they have health insurance, which is only affordable through employer plans. Unemployment compensation provides a small fraction of previous income for only a short time and only under certain circumstances. The case of Enrique Morones dramatically demonstrates the price of advocacy that conflicts with an employer's attitude. But the same kind of pressure for economic conformity is evident in the lives of Carrie and Mary Dann, the Charleston Five, Lynne Stewart and Chokwe Lumumba.

In the United States, income is the measure of vulnerability. For all the vast wealth of the United States, the prime mover of human rights abuse continues to be the disparity between those who have—wealth, resources, education, information—and those who do not. No matter how grievous the offense, wealth protects against consequence; no matter how trivial the offense, poverty invites prosecution. One of the triumphs of the human rights defenders in this report is that they choose to live in the same way as the people they protect.

6. Nature of Human Rights Defender Work

"...[W]hen the rights of human rights defenders are violated, all our rights are put in jeopardy and all of us are made less safe"
—UN Secretary General Kofi Annan

For several of the defenders presented here, motivation and purpose springs from early exposure to inspirational exemplars. Chokwe Lumumba cites Malcolm X; Enrique Morones mentions Cesar Chavez and his own grandfather; Charles Tisdale credits his mother; nearly all the defenders refer to the life and death of Martin Luther King.

Others draw from their own experience enduring the kind of abuse they now defend. Cheri Honkala was homeless before she became an advocate for the homeless and a defender of economic and social rights. Most of the Charleston Five became fully committed to lives of labor advocacy after being beaten and imprisoned for their activism. Both Brenda and Wanda Henson were married to abusive husbands, had children while very young and lived through custody battles; they later used their experience to advocate for other mothers deserving custody of their children. The Immokalee Workers are able to penetrate the world of forced labor because most of them suffered within it.

Still others followed a spiritual path to advocacy. Carrie and Mary Dann repeatedly assert that they cannot practice their beliefs if they are separated from the land. James Yee found his way to advocacy through Islam, Jeff Dietrich through Christianity. All the defenders are driven by something other than the expectation of reward or even progress: a moral and ethical inability to stand by and do nothing while other people suffer violations of their rights as human beings.

Many of the defenders in this report and many more of their associates have found new motivation, new strategies and new ways of thinking by adopting and adapting international human rights language, guarantees and protections, and by appealing to international human rights forums about violations in the United States. Cheri Honkala, the Kensington Welfare Rights Union and the Poor People's Campaign for Economic Human Rights have based their action program explicitly within the framework of international human rights provisions. Enrique Morones uses territorial agreements between the USA and Mexico to make his case for preventing the disintegration of Latino families crossing the border. Carrie and Mary Dann have taken their appeal for indigenous and land rights to the appropriate forums at the United Nations, the Organization of American States and the Inter-American Court on Human Rights, resulting in a ruling that the US Government had indeed violated their rights. Chokwe Lumumba, following the example of Martin Luther King, has been speaking in terms of human rights since 1968. James Yee and Farouk Abdel-Muhti have been incarcerated at least partly because of their defense of the international human rights of people who are imprisoned without charge.

B. Human Rights Defenders: Protections, Laws and Recourse

1. US Law

United States law provides significant protections to human rights activists, advocates and defenders, and offers various mechanisms for redress. The First and Fourteenth Amendments to the US Constitution effectively guarantee freedom to document, comment on, distribute, and seek redress for human rights violations. They assure that activists have the unfettered right to join together and form associations for the purpose of advancing their cause.

Any "person" may bring a lawsuit in federal court if their rights under the US Constitution have been violated. US law also provides remedies for employment discrimination and the right to organize and engage in peaceful labor activities. Though not perfect, the body of US civil rights legislation, complemented by state and local legislation, is comprehensive and functions effectively in general.

There are gaps in this system of protection, some of which are exemplified by the case studies in this report. Too often court or administrative proceedings may reflect the prejudices of the society at large. The court system may also be out of reach for many of the most vulnerable in society and the judiciary has become more resistant to claims of individual rights in recent years.

The willingness of the US Justice Department to use its authority to enforce civil rights laws by criminal or civil proceedings varies greatly. The Justice Department has substantial authority, *inter alia*, to address problems of prison abuse, police abuse and slavery-like conditions. The Justice Department could use this authority much more aggressively.

Missing from US law, however, is any specific reference to protection of human rights defenders similar to that offered by the UN Declaration on Human Rights Defenders. In general, US law enforces international human rights standards only to the extent such standards are already codified in US law.

2. State Law

Most US states also offer complementary protections and avenues of redress for human rights defenders. Most states have constitutions which recognize basic rights necessary to advocates: freedom of speech, freedom of assembly, and the right to petition the Government for redress of grievances. Courts in most states have found that advocacy is protected by the US Constitution. It appears that no US state has a statute devoted specifically to human rights defenders.

Civil rights laws in California, for example, are administered by the Department of Fair Employment and Housing; it is meant to promote civil rights legislation, adjudicate complaints that can be addressed administratively and enforce housing regulations. California Civil Code 52.1 "protects all people within the state from interference with the free exercise or enjoyment of the rights guaranteed them by the state or the United States". Many other states have similar laws and administrative enforcement bodies.

3. International Protections

The United States has ratified The Convention Against Torture and Other Cruel, Inhuman or Degrading Treatment or Punishment; the International Covenant on Civil and Political Rights; and the International Convention on the Elimination of All Forms of Racial Discrimination. It has done so subject to limitations that have been widely criticized by the international community. The US has signed but not ratified the Convention on the Elimination of All Forms of Discrimination Against Women, the American Convention on Human Rights and the International Covenant on Economic, Social and Cultural Rights.

The United States has provided initial reports under the treaties it has ratified. It has not agreed to respond to any individual complaints. However, these treaties do not appear to have a significant impact on human rights protections within the United States.

Human Rights Defenders

"Domestic implementation of human rights standards largely depends on the ability of individuals and groups to promote and protect human rights and to pressure their governments to live up to their legal obligations. By documenting and exposing human rights violations and holding governments accountable, by seeking remedies for victims and educating populations on their human rights, these individuals — commonly referred to as 'human rights defenders' — play a crucial role in combating violations and improving human rights situations" — Lawyers Committee for Human Rights[102]

On December 9, 1998, the United Nations adopted the Declaration on Human Rights Defenders, a landmark in the protection of those who are in jeopardy as a result of their advocacy. Adopted with the formal title "Declaration on the Rights and Responsibilities of Individuals, Groups and Organs of Society to Promote and Protect Universally Recognized Human Rights and Fundamental Freedoms", it is the first UN document affirming

---

[102] Lawyers Committee for Human Rights (1999), *Protecting Human Rights Defenders: Analysis of the Newly Adopted Declaration on Human Rights Defenders*, Washington DC: LCHR.

the significance of the work of human rights defenders and the necessity of protecting them.

During its 2000 session, the UN Commission on Human Rights established the position of Special Representative of the Secretary-General on human rights defenders. The Special Representative is charged with responsibility for pressing implementation of the provisions in the Declaration on Human Rights Defenders.

The Declaration states that:

- Everyone has the right to promote, protect and defend human rights.
- Human rights defenders are most vulnerable to attacks on their rights to peaceful assembly, to form and join non-governmental organizations, to provide information, and to seek redress from national and international authorities.
- Everyone is entitled to full protection against retaliation for exercising human rights.
- States are required to implement human rights in law and in practice.
- States are obliged to protect human rights defenders from reprisals.
- States have the responsibility to investigate allegations of violations.

Recommendations

Front Line believes that the case studies in this Report reflect the kinds of challenges that many human rights defenders face in their work in the United States. Though human rights defenders enjoy a wide range of protections in the United States, the promises made in the Declaration on Human Rights Defenders are not uniformly respected and further action needs to be taken to make these promises a universal reality for all human rights defenders in the United States.

The work of these human rights defenders also reveals the gaps in human rights protection in the United States more generally. This is especially true for the most vulnerable segments of American society. Though US law provides many human rights protections, the United States has not taken seriously its commitment to the universal and indivisible international human rights standards set forth in the Universal Declaration of Human Rights and the body of international human rights treaties the international community has agreed on since World War Two. In particular, the United States refuses to recognize international economic, social and cultural rights as rights.

Thus, Front Line starts with a recommendation that all levels of government in the United States take steps to fully implement the rights recognized in the human rights treaties the United States has ratified and to complete the process of ratification and implementation of the full range of civil, political, economic, social and cultural rights promised by the Universal Declaration of Human Rights. All persons in the United States will enjoy greater protection and freedoms if such steps are taken.

With respect to human rights defenders, in particular, Front Line makes the following recommendations based on the research in this Report:

1. At all levels of government in the USA, federal, state and local, steps should be taken to implement the protections in the UN Human Rights Defenders Declaration. These steps should include legislative, administrative and judicial actions.

2. The Civil Rights Division of the US Justice Department should use its existing powers to investigate allegations of violations of the rights of

human rights defenders and should seek additional authority and resources to the extent necessary to ensure that the protections in the Human Rights Defender Declaration are fulfilled.

3. Other federal agencies (e.g. the Department of Homeland Security) should take similar steps to ensure that the rights of human rights defenders are respected in the course of their activities.

4. Congress should hold hearings on the impact of measures taken in pursuit of the "war against terrorism" (e.g. political surveillance, intrusions on privacy, detention policies) on the work of human rights defenders in the United States and take action to protect human rights defenders in this context.

5. State and local law enforcement and prosecutorial agencies should take similar steps to ensure the fulfillment of the protections in the Human Rights Defender Declaration in their jurisdictions. These actions should include steps to protect human rights defenders from violence and other forms of harassment by private parties as well. As this Report demonstrates, there are some states (e.g. Mississippi) where such actions must be undertaken on an urgent basis.

6. The U.S. Civil Rights Commission should investigate the extent to which the protections in the Human Rights Defenders Declaration are being fulfilled within the United States and should recommend legislative and administrative reforms to ensure the nationwide implementation of the Declaration.

7. The United States should invite the UN Special Representative for Human Rights Defenders to visit the United States and to report on the state of protections for human rights defenders.

8. Human rights NGOs in other countries should consider taking action in support of human rights defenders at risk in the United States.

9. Human rights NGOs in and outside the United States should consider joint projects and exchanges ensuring that human rights defenders in the United States become active participants in the international human rights movement. Front Line believes that the exchange of experiences across boundaries will benefit all human rights defenders.

Human Rights Defenders in the United States
Conclusion

Each of the human rights defenders profiled in this report has demonstrated extraordinary courage, commitment and capacity in the face of threats, harassment, intimidation and abuse. Some have been denied their ability to earn a living. Some have been beaten and threatened with death. Some have been detained and imprisoned, held without charge or held in solitary confinement. All have more than enough reason to abandon their advocacy.

Yet all continue to defend, promote and protect human rights and human rights defenders. They deserve our appreciation and admiration. They deserve the cooperation and protection of the US Government. They deserve the embrace and support of the international community of human rights defenders. And they deserve our own active participation in the movement for universal human rights.

The human rights defenders represented in this report are all working to promote a vision of the inextricable integration of all human rights: economic, social and cultural as well as civil and political. And each of them has experienced consequences and repercussions that are economic and social as well as civil and political. Taken together, they are walking manifestations of the essential indivisibility of all human rights.

Each of the human rights defenders profiled in this report stands in for uncounted and unrecognized legions of activists and advocates who continually demonstrate the courage, capacity, strength and faith required to serve vulnerable communities, to protect other activists, and to promote respect for human rights in the United States.

We hope that the ideas and methods employed by these human rights defenders will prove useful to other advocates and activists in the US and in other countries. We hope that this report will give human rights defenders throughout the world a sense of solidarity with, and support for, their colleagues in the United States. And we hope that the lives and the work of the individuals presented here will serve as models for human rights activists and advocates around the world as they become human rights defenders.

The United States of America is fortunate to have human rights advocates such as James Yee and Farouk Abdel-Muhti; Lynne Stewart and Chokwe Lumumba; Cheri Honkala and Jeff Dietrich; the Charleston Five and the Coalition of Immokalee Workers; Carrie and Mary Dann; Brenda and Wanda Henson; Charles Tisdale and Enrique Morones.

We applaud their work and wish them continued success and freedom from interference, and we commit ourselves to supporting them.

Appendix I

United Nations Declaration on the Right and Responsibility of Individuals, Groups and Organs of Society to Promote and Protect Universally Recognized Human Rights and Fundamental Freedoms

General Assembly resolution 53/144

The General Assembly,

Reaffirming the importance of the observance of the purposes and principles of the Charter of the United Nations for the promotion and protection of all human rights and fundamental freedoms for all persons in all countries of the world,

Taking note of Commission on Human Rights resolution 1998/7 of 3 April 1998, See *Official Records of the Economic and Social Council, 1998, Supplement No. 3* (E/1998/23), chap. II, sect. A. in which the Commission approved the text of the draft declaration on the right and responsibility of individuals, groups and organs of society to promote and protect universally recognized human rights and fundamental freedoms,

Taking note also of Economic and Social Council resolution 1998/33 of 30 July 1998, in which the Council recommended the draft declaration to the General Assembly for adoption,

Conscious of the importance of the adoption of the draft declaration in the context of the fiftieth anniversary of the Universal Declaration of Human Rights, Resolution 217 A (III).

1. *Adopts* the Declaration on the Right and Responsibility of Individuals, Groups and Organs of Society to Promote and Protect Universally Recognized Human Rights and Fundamental Freedoms, annexed to the present resolution;

2. *Invites* Governments, agencies and organizations of the United Nations system and intergovernmental and non-governmental organizations to intensify their efforts to disseminate the Declaration and to promote universal respect and understanding thereof, and requests the Secretary-General to include the text of the Declaration in the next edition of *Human Rights: A Compilation of International Instruments.*

85th plenary meeting
9 December 1998

ANNEX
Declaration on the Right and Responsibility of Individuals, Groups and Organs of Society to Promote and Protect Universally Recognized Human Rights and Fundamental Freedoms

The General Assembly,

Reaffirming the importance of the observance of the purposes and principles of the Charter of the United Nations for the promotion and protection of all human rights and fundamental freedoms for all persons in all countries of the world,

Reaffirming also the importance of the Universal Declaration of Human Rights[2] and the International Covenants on Human Rights Resolution 2200 A (XXI), annex. As basic elements of international efforts to promote universal respect for and observance of human rights and fundamental freedoms and the importance of other human rights instruments adopted within the United Nations system, as well as those at the regional level,

Stressing that all members of the international community shall fulfil, jointly and separately, their solemn obligation to promote and encourage respect for human rights and fundamental freedoms for all without distinction of any kind, including distinctions based on race, colour, sex, language, religion, political or other opinion, national or social origin, property, birth or other status, and reaffirming the particular importance of achieving international cooperation to fulfil this obligation according to the Charter,

Acknowledging the important role of international cooperation for, and the valuable work of individuals, groups and associations in contributing to, the effective elimination of all violations of human rights and fundamental freedoms of peoples and individuals, including in relation to mass, flagrant or systematic violations such as those resulting from apartheid, all forms of racial discrimination, colonialism, foreign domination or occupation, aggression or threats to national sovereignty, national unity or territorial integrity and from the refusal to recognize the right of peoples to self-determination and the right of every people to exercise full sovereignty over its wealth and natural resources,

Recognizing the relationship between international peace and security and the enjoyment of human rights and fundamental freedoms, and mindful that

174

the absence of international peace and security does not excuse non-compliance,

Reiterating that all human rights and fundamental freedoms are universal, indivisible, interdependent and interrelated and should be promoted and implemented in a fair and equitable manner, without prejudice to the implementation of each of those rights and freedoms,

Stressing that the prime responsibility and duty to promote and protect human rights and fundamental freedoms lie with the State,

Recognizing the right and the responsibility of individuals, groups and associations to promote respect for and foster knowledge of human rights and fundamental freedoms at the national and international levels,

Declares:

Article 1

Everyone has the right, individually and in association with others, to promote and to strive for the protection and realization of human rights and fundamental freedoms at the national and international levels.

Article 2

1. Each State has a prime responsibility and duty to protect, promote and implement all human rights and fundamental freedoms, *inter alia*, by adopting such steps as may be necessary to create all conditions necessary in the social, economic, political and other fields, as well as the legal guarantees required to ensure that all persons under its jurisdiction, individually and in association with others, are able to enjoy all those rights and freedoms in practice.

2. Each State shall adopt such legislative, administrative and other steps as may be necessary to ensure that the rights and freedoms referred to in the present Declaration are effectively guaranteed.

Article 3

Domestic law consistent with the Charter of the United Nations and other international obligations of the State in the field of human rights and fundamental freedoms is the juridical framework within which human rights and fundamental freedoms should be implemented and enjoyed and within which all activities referred to in the present Declaration for the promotion, protection and effective realization of those rights and freedoms should be conducted.

Article 4

Nothing in the present Declaration shall be construed as impairing or contradicting the purposes and principles of the Charter of the United Nations or as restricting or derogating from the provisions of the Universal Declaration of Human Rights, the International Covenants on Human Rights[3] and other international instruments and commitments applicable in this field.

Article 5

For the purpose of promoting and protecting human rights and fundamental freedoms, everyone has the right, individually and in association with others, at the national and international levels:

(*a*) To meet or assemble peacefully;

(*b*) To form, join and participate in non-governmental organizations, associations or groups;

(*c*) To communicate with non-governmental or intergovernmental organizations.

Article 6

Everyone has the right, individually and in association with others:

(*a*) To know, seek, obtain, receive and hold information about all human rights and fundamental freedoms, including having access to information as to how those rights and freedoms are given effect in domestic legislative, judicial or administrative systems;

(*b*) As provided for in human rights and other applicable international instruments, freely to publish, impart or disseminate to others views, information and knowledge on all human rights and fundamental freedoms;

(*c*) To study, discuss, form and hold opinions on the observance, both in law and in practice, of all human rights and fundamental freedoms and, through these and other appropriate means, to draw public attention to those matters.

Article 7

Everyone has the right, individually and in association with others, to develop and discuss new human rights ideas and principles and to advocate their acceptance.

Article 8

1. Everyone has the right, individually and in association with others, to have effective access, on a non-discriminatory basis, to participation in the government of his or her country and in the conduct of public affairs.

2. This includes, *inter alia*, the right, individually and in association with others, to submit to governmental bodies and agencies and organizations concerned with public affairs criticism and proposals for improving their functioning and to draw attention to any aspect of their work that may hinder or impede the promotion, protection and realization of human rights and fundamental freedoms.

Article 9

1. In the exercise of human rights and fundamental freedoms, including the promotion and protection of human rights as referred to in the present Declaration; everyone has the right, individually and in association with others, to benefit from an effective remedy and to be protected in the event of the violation of those rights.

2. To this end, everyone whose rights or freedoms are allegedly violated has the right, either in person or through legally authorized representation, to complain to and have that complaint promptly reviewed in a public hearing before an independent, impartial and competent judicial or other authority

established by law and to obtain from such an authority a decision, in accordance with law, providing redress, including any compensation due, where there has been a violation of that person's rights or freedoms, as well as enforcement of the eventual decision and award, all without undue delay.

3. To the same end, everyone has the right, individually and in association with others, *inter alia*:

(a) To complain about the policies and actions of individual officials and governmental bodies with regard to violations of human rights and fundamental freedoms, by petition or other appropriate means, to competent domestic judicial, administrative or legislative authorities or any other competent authority provided for by the legal system of the State, which should render their decision on the complaint without undue delay;

(*b*) To attend public hearings, proceedings and trials so as to form an opinion on their compliance with national law and applicable international obligations and commitments;

(*c*) To offer and provide professionally qualified legal assistance or other relevant advice and assistance in defending human rights and fundamental freedoms.

4. To the same end, and in accordance with applicable international instruments and procedures, everyone has the right, individually and in association with others, to unhindered access to and communication with international bodies with general or special competence to receive and consider communications on matters of human rights and fundamental freedoms.

5. The State shall conduct a prompt and impartial investigation or ensure that an inquiry takes place whenever there is reasonable ground to believe that a violation of human rights and fundamental freedoms has occurred in any territory under its jurisdiction.

Article 10

No one shall participate, by act or by failure to act where required, in violating human rights and fundamental freedoms and no one shall be subjected to punishment or adverse action of any kind for refusing to do so.

Article 11

Everyone has the right, individually and in association with others, to the lawful exercise of his or her occupation or profession. Everyone who, as a result of his or her profession, can affect the human dignity, human rights and fundamental freedoms of others should respect those rights and freedoms and comply with relevant national and international standards of occupational and professional conduct or ethics.

Article 12

1. Everyone has the right, individually and in association with others, to participate in peaceful activities against violations of human rights and fundamental freedoms.

2. The State shall take all necessary measures to ensure the protection by the competent authorities of everyone, individually and in association with others, against any violence, threats, retaliation, de facto or *de jure* adverse discrimination, pressure or any other arbitrary action as a consequence of his or her legitimate exercise of the rights referred to in the present Declaration.

3. In this connection, everyone is entitled, individually and in association with others, to be protected effectively under national law in reacting against or opposing, through peaceful means, activities and acts, including those by omission, attributable to States that result in violations of human rights and fundamental freedoms, as well as acts of violence perpetrated by groups or individuals that affect the enjoyment of human rights and fundamental freedoms.

Article 13

Everyone has the right, individually and in association with others, to solicit, receive and utilize resources for the express purpose of promoting and protecting human rights and fundamental freedoms through peaceful means, in accordance with article 3 of the present Declaration.

Article 14

1. The State has the responsibility to take legislative, judicial, and administrative or other appropriate measures to promote the understanding

by all persons under its jurisdiction of their civil, political, economic, social and cultural rights.

2. Such measures shall include, *inter alia*:

(a) The publication and widespread availability of national laws and regulations and of applicable basic international human rights instruments;

(b) Full and equal access to international documents in the field of human rights, including the periodic reports by the State to the bodies established by the international human rights treaties to which it is a party, as well as the summary records of discussions and the official reports of these bodies.

3. The State shall ensure and support, where appropriate, the creation and development of further independent national institutions for the promotion and protection of human rights and fundamental freedoms in all territory under its jurisdiction, whether they be ombudsmen, human rights commissions or any other form of national institution.

Article 15

The State has the responsibility to promote and facilitate the teaching of human rights and fundamental freedoms at all levels of education and to ensure that all those responsible for training lawyers, law enforcement officers, the personnel of the armed forces and public officials include appropriate elements of human rights teaching in their training programme.

Article 16

Individuals, non-governmental organizations and relevant institutions have an important role to play in contributing to making the public more aware of questions relating to all human rights and fundamental freedoms through activities such as education, training and research in these areas to strengthen further, *inter alia*, understanding, tolerance, peace and friendly relations among nations and among all racial and religious groups, bearing in mind the various backgrounds of the societies and communities in which they carry out their activities.

Article 17

In the exercise of the rights and freedoms referred to in the present Declaration, everyone, acting individually and in association with others, shall be subject only to such limitations as are in accordance with applicable international obligations and are determined by law solely for the purpose of securing due recognition and respect for the rights and freedoms of others and of meeting the just requirements of morality, public order and the general welfare in a democratic society.

Article 18

1. Everyone has duties towards and within the community, in which alone the free and full development of his or her personality is possible.

2. Individuals, groups, institutions and non-governmental organizations have an important role to play and a responsibility in safeguarding democracy, promoting human rights and fundamental freedoms and contributing to the promotion and advancement of democratic societies, institutions and processes.

3. Individuals, groups, institutions and non-governmental organizations also have an important role and a responsibility in contributing, as appropriate, to the promotion of the right of everyone to a social and international order in which the rights and freedoms set forth in the Universal Declaration of Human Rights and other human rights instruments can be fully realized.

Article 19

Nothing in the present Declaration shall be interpreted as implying for any individual, group or organ of society or any State the right to engage in any activity or to perform any act aimed at the destruction of the rights and freedoms referred to in the present Declaration.

Article 20

Nothing in the present Declaration shall be interpreted as permitting States to support and promote activities of individuals, groups of individuals, institutions or non-governmental organizations contrary to the provisions of the Charter of the United Nations.

Appendix II
Additional International Protections

Equal Treatment and Non-Discrimination

Internationally, equal treatment under the law is required by the United Nations Charter, the Universal Declaration of Human Rights (UDHR), and the International Covenant on Civil and Political Rights (ICCPR). Article 2 of the UDHR states that none of the rights in the rest of the Declaration can be limited by race or color; discrimination of any kind on any right, including economic, social and cultural rights, is a violation. Equal treatment protections are more specifically provided in Article 6 of the UDHR, Article 16 of the ICCPR, and Article 3 of the American Convention on Human Rights.

More guidelines are contained in the Convention to Eliminate Racial Discrimination (CERD). In article 2, CERD affirms that, "States Parties condemn racial discrimination and undertake to pursue by all appropriate means and without delay a policy of eliminating racial discrimination in all its forms and promoting understanding among all races..."

Freedom of Thought, Speech, Assembly and Protest

Articles 18, 19 and 20 of the UDHR guarantee freedom of thought, speech, assembly and peaceful protest. Article 18 of the ICCPR expands on the rights established in the UDHR.

Personal Security

Taken together, articles 3, 5 and 9 of the UDHR provide for the protection of personal security, the right not to be harmed or killed. Article 4 of the ICCPR guarantees security of person and fair treatment. Article 4 warns that the basic human rights contained in Articles 6, 7, 8, 11, 15, 16 and 18 are so fundamental that they cannot be abrogated even in times of war.

Sexual Identity

Sexual identity as a right requiring protection has not been explicitly articulated in basic human rights documents, and no international covenant guarantees sexual identity rights. Article 26 of the ICCPR establishes that discrimination based on sex or other status is not allowed.

Detention and Imprisonment

Freedom from arbitrary detention and detention without charge has a prominent place in international human rights documents. Article 9 of the UDHR sets forth freedom from arbitrary detention, arrest or exile. In the ICCPR, Articles 9 through 12 define the necessary legal procedures for someone being charged with a crime, state that no one may be held without being charged, and hold that arrested persons must be treated with respect for their human dignity.

In 1988 the UN issued the "Body of Principles for the Protection of All Persons under Any Form of Detention or Imprisonment". Especially relevant to US conditions are:

Principle 6: "No person under any form of detention or imprisonment shall be subjected to torture or to cruel, inhuman or degrading treatment or punishment. No circumstance whatever may be invoked as a justification for torture or other cruel, inhuman or degrading treatment or punishment." In an explanatory note on this principle, the document says, "The term 'cruel, inhuman or degrading treatment or punishment' should be interpreted so as to extend the widest possible protection against abuses, whether physical or mental, including the holding of a detained or imprisoned person in conditions which deprive him, temporarily or permanently, of the use of any of his natural senses, such as sight or hearing, or of his awareness of place and the passing of time".

Principle 11: "A person shall not be kept in detention without being given an effective opportunity to be heard promptly by a judicial or other authority."

In 1990 the UN issued its "Basic Principles for the Treatment of Prisoners". Article 1 holds that, "All prisoners shall be treated with respect due to their inherent dignity and value as human beings". Article 2 states, "There shall be no discrimination on the grounds of race, color, sex, language, religion, political or other opinion, national or social origin, property, birth or other status". Article 3 advises that, "It is, however, desirable to respect the religious beliefs and cultural precepts of the group to which prisoners belong, whenever local conditions so require". Article 5 says in part,

183

"Except for those limitations that are demonstrably necessitated by the fact of incarceration, all prisoners shall retain the human rights and fundamental freedoms set out in the Universal Declaration of Human Rights". Finally, Article 9 provides that, "Prisoners shall have access to the health services available in the country without discrimination on the grounds of their legal situation".

Housing

Economic and social human rights are presented in Article 25 of the UDHR, including the right to adequate housing. Article 11 of the International Covenant on Economic, Social and Cultural Rights (ICESCR) provides for the right to adequate housing for the individual and the family. The USA has yet to ratify the ICESCR. The International Labor Organization (ILO) has taken responsibility for setting international standards of economic and social rights and for creating mechanisms for implementation.

Native Americans

Native Americans and other indigenous groups are afforded protections through the UDHR and the ICCPR. But specific rights are guaranteed to the individual rather than the group. Article 27 of the ICCPR warrants that ethnic minorities may practice their culture, language and religion without interference by the state. Native Americans and other indigenous peoples have sought independence based on the sovereignty rights recognized in the UN Charter and the UDHR.

In 1962 the UN General Assembly passed a resolution on permanent sovereignty over natural resources, which declares that, "The right of peoples and nations to permanent sovereignty over their natural wealth and resources must be exercised in the interest of their national development and the well-being of the people of the State concerned".

In 1992 the UN General Assembly adopted the Declaration on the Rights of Persons Belonging to National or Ethnic, Religious and Linguistic Minorities.

Article 1 holds that, "States shall protect the existence and the national or ethnic, cultural, religious and linguistic identity of minorities within their respective territories and shall encourage conditions for the promotion of that identity".

Article 2 states that, "Persons belonging to national or ethnic, religious or linguistic minorities have the right to enjoy their own culture, to profess and practice their own religion, and to use their own language, in private or in public, freely and without interference or any form of discrimination".
Significantly, Article 3 make the case for group rights: "Persons belonging to minorities may exercise their rights, including those set forth in the present Declaration, individually as well as in community with other members of their group, without any discrimination".

Article 4 requires states to do more than passively accept these rights: "States shall take measures where required to ensure that persons belonging to minorities may exercise fully and effectively all their human rights and fundamental freedoms without any discrimination and in full equality before the law".

Immigration

International law does not provide immigrants with the same rights as citizens of the country of destination, especially not for immigrants who move "of their own will". However, immigrants are guaranteed fundamental human rights such as freedom from harm, freedom of speech and assembly, and the right to a fair trial. Moreover, such basic human rights are not bound to states but are attached to individuals, including immigrants.

Slavery

The forms of forced labor and slavery are defined in the "Supplementary Convention on the Abolition of Slavery, the Slave Trade, and Institutions and Practices Similar to Slavery", adopted by the UN in 1956. The definition of slavery is expanded to include debt bondage, serfdom, and the exploitation of children. Further guarantees are contained in the American Convention on Human Rights, signed in 1969. Article 6 of the ACHR states, "No one shall be subjected to slavery or to involuntary servitude, which are prohibited in all their forms, as are the slave trade and traffic in women", and, "No one shall be required to perform forced or compulsory labor. Article 8 of the ICCPR directly prohibits forced or compulsory labor.

Migrant Labor

In 1990, the UN adopted the International Convention on the Protection of the Rights of All Migrant Workers and Members of Their Families. Article 10 states, "No migrant worker or member of his or her family shall be subjected to torture or to cruel, inhuman or degrading treatment or punishment". Article 11 holds that, "No migrant worker or member of his or her family shall be held in slavery or servitude", and "No migrant worker or member of his or her family shall be required to perform forced or compulsory labor", Article 14 says, "No migrant worker or member of his or her family shall be subjected to arbitrary or unlawful interference with his or her privacy, family, home, correspondence or other communications, or to unlawful attacks on his or her honor and reputation".

Law Enforcement

In 1979, the UN issued a Code of Conduct for Law Enforcement Officials. Article 2 states, "In the performance of their duty, law enforcement officials shall respect and protect human dignity and maintain and uphold the human rights of all persons".

Appendix III
Special Representative of the Secretary General on human rights defenders

In August 2000, Ms. Hina Jilani was asked by Secretary General Kofi Annan to become the first holder of the position of Special Representative of the Secretary General on human rights defenders, in accordance with the provisions of Commission on Human Rights resolution E/CN.4/RES/2000/61, of 26 April 2000. Ms. Jilani's initial remit of 3 years was renewed by a subsequent Commission resolution in April 2003 (E/CN.4/RES/2003/64).

Hina Jilani is an Advocate of the Supreme Court of Pakistan and has been a human rights defender for many years, working in particular in favour of the rights of women, minorities and children. Ms. Jilani was a co-founder of the first all-women law firm in Pakistan in 1980. She also founded Pakistan's first legal aid center in 1986. She is based in Lahore, Pakistan.

Human rights defenders in the US and around the world can make complaints to the Special Representative. The procedure for making complaints is on the Special Representative's webpage http://www.unhchr.ch/defenders/complaints.htm.

The UN Human Rights Defenders Office can be contacted directly:

UN Special Representative on human rights defenders
Office of the High Commissioner of Human Rights

Palais Wilson
8-14 Avenue de la Paix
1211 Geneva 10, Switzerland
Telephone: (41-22) 917-9000 Callers should ask for the staff supporting the mandate of the Special Representative on human rights defenders.
Fax: +41 22 917 9006
urgent-action@ohchr.org The text of the e-mail should refer to the human rights defenders mandate.